How to Invest in Canadian Securities

Toronto
Vancouver
Calgary
Montreal
Halifax

Names of individual securities mentioned in this text are for purposes of example only and are not to be construed as recommendations for purchase or sale.

Prices of individual securities given in this text are for the purposes of comparison and illustration only and were approximate figures for the period when the text was being prepared. Current quotations may be obtained from the financial pages of daily newspapers or the financial press or from your Investment Advisor.

While information contained in this text has been obtained from sources the publisher believes to be reliable, it cannot be guaranteed nor does it purport to treat each subject exhaustively.

This publication is designed to provide accurate and authoritative information in regard to the subjects covered. It is distributed with the understanding that the Canadian Securities Institute and the Investor Learning Centre of Canada are not engaged in rendering legal, accounting or other professional service. If legal advice or other expert assistance is required, the services of competent professional persons should be sought.

Canadian Cataloguing in Publication Data

Main entry under title:

How to invest in Canadian Securities

Rev. ed.
ISBN 1-894289-56-0

1. Securities-Canada. I. Canadian Securities Institute.

HG5152.H69 2000 332.63'2'0971 C00-930740-0

First Printing 1970 by the Canadian Securities Institute.
Revised and Reprinted 1978, 1984, 1986, 1988, 1994, 1997, 2000.

 Printed and bound in Canada

CANADIAN SECURITIES INSTITUTE 121 King Street West, Suite 1550, Toronto, Ontario M5H 3T9
Tel: (416) 364-9130 Fax: (416) 359-0486 internet: www.csi.ca

Table of Contents

Other titles in this series

Bottom Line Guide to Investing
(ISBN 0-919796-57-5)

How to Read Financial Statements
(ISBN 1-894289-57-9)

How to Start and Run an Investment Club
(ISBN 1-894289-04-8)

What every Canadian should know about Mutual Funds
(ISBN 1-894289-69-2)

What every Canadian should know about Family Finance
(ISBN 1-894289-70-6)

Investment Terms & Definitions
(ISBN 1-894289-03-X)

Still strong after 30 years

For millions of Canadians today, learning to invest has become as much a part of life as learning to drive a car. We are increasingly being pushed to become more financially self-reliant. More and more, it is up to us to finance a bigger slice of our children's education and our retirements. We must make crucial decisions today that will impact the very standard of living we and our children will enjoy in the future.

And yet, how many of us can truly say we are fully prepared for these important choices that confront us? Without the benefit of a formal education in investing, most of us either err on the side of caution or inadvertently risk more than we are prepared to. Many of us live in worry and doubt about whether we've potentially made the wrong choices. We lack confidence in our advisors, in government programs and, ultimately, in ourselves.

But now you are about to change all of that with this book. You are going to gain confidence about the future. You will learn what you need to make informed investment decisions, either on your own or with the help of a professional advisor. What you'll read is distilled from more than three decades of knowledge at the Canadian Securities Institute (CSI), the national securities industry educator.

But this isn't an academic text. It's a practical, hands-on guide (for the rest of us). Its objective is to give you the confidence that comes from a deeper understanding of your available investment choices. Since it was first published in 1964, many thousands of people have used it to broaden their understanding of investing in

Canada. It is widely employed in college programs, by financial planners and investment professionals, and most of all by ordinary investors.

We have organized the book along product lines. After a tour of the Canadian capital markets and the securities industry, you will learn about bonds, stocks, investment funds and options. The final chapter helps you (know how to) build your own investment portfolio by pulling together what you have learned about the main types of investments.

While it's best to take the time to read the entire book, you can pick only those chapters you're most interested in. Of course, even if you read the whole book, you will likely want to refer back to refresh your memory of specific details. This should be easy since we've clearly sign-posted all the information under descriptive headings and included a detailed index at the back.

And since no up-to-date investment guide would be complete without referring to Internet resources available to you to expand your knowledge, we've included these in the text. You will also find useful tips to help you avoid the pitfalls of online investing. There's also new material on clone funds and segregated funds, and on a low-cost alternative to mutual funds: index participation units.

Finally, we would like to credit the many people who have contributed to this book over the past three decades. Their names are too numerous to list here, but their wisdom and knowledge are found on every page. Unique for this edition is the guidance and plain language expertise provided by the development team of the Investor Learning Centre of Canada.

Most of all, continuing inspiration for new editions of the book comes from the thousands of Canadians who write, call or visit the Canadian Securities Institute and the Investor Learning Centre looking to learn more about investing. It is your continued endorsement of us as the best sources of investment information that makes it possible to offer resources such as this book.

Investing and the Capital Markets

Where companies that need capital meet investors who have it.

The Capital Market

You might think you know absolutely nothing about investing? But you probably know more than you take credit for. At the very least, you know that you can invest in many things, including real estate, securities, stamps, coins and works of art.

This book is about one type of investment: securities. Securities take several forms, including stocks, bonds, mutual funds and options.

Over the next 209 pages, you'll take a look at some of the most important aspects about investing in securities – like how the securities system works, what stocks and bonds are, how to analyze securities, and how to build an investment portfolio.

But let's start at the beginning...

So that's where my money goes!

When you buy and sell securities, you are taking part in the capital market. Capital is another word for money, such as your savings. The capital market isn't a place. It's a collection of markets, organizations and products. Through it, people or institutions with money to invest are brought together with those who need money.

When you invest, you are supplying capital to individuals, businesses and governments for many key social and economic uses. As such, your investment may pay off for you in two ways: first, by making you money; and second, by improving our economy and our country as a whole.

There are two main sources of capital: individuals and institutions. Individuals are people like you. In fact, you almost certainly already supply money to the capital market. You're a supplier if you have a bank account. The bank loans the money you deposit to other people and to businesses. You may also be providing capital directly to businesses or governments by investing in their securities. When you buy a Canada Savings Bond for instance, you're supplying capital to the government.

You may also be an indirect source of capital through an institution. Institutional investors are an important source of capital. They include banks, life insurance companies, pension funds, and mutual funds. If you are a member of a company pension plan, your money is pooled with co-workers' and then invested in the capital markets.

You're a supplier of capital if you buy a Canada Savings Bond.

You're also most likely a user of capital. If you have a mortgage on your house, if you have ever taken out a car loan or if you sometimes carry a balance on your credit card, you are using other people's money.

Similarly, businesses use other people's money to help fund their operations. Of course, some of the largest and most consistent borrowers of capital over the years have been the various levels of government. Governments borrow money when the taxes they collect aren't enough to cover their spending.

The three levels of government – federal, provincial and municipal – use the money they borrow for several things. They pay for capital projects, like building roads, hospitals, and schools; for social services like welfare; and for interest on money they've already borrowed.

Where stocks and bonds come from

In the capital market, securities are used as evidence of a financial transaction between suppliers and users of capital. The security outlines the transaction's details, like how much money is involved and what each party's rights and obligations are.

There are two main types of securities transactions: lending money, and buying an ownership interest in a company. When the security is for a loan, it's called a debt instrument. When it's for an ownership stake, it's called an equity security.

Governments and businesses generally borrow money by issuing debt instruments such as bonds and debentures. When you buy a bond, you are lending money to the bond's issuer, be it a government or corporation. The issuer promises to repay you the principal (the amount borrowed) at the end of the loan period and pay you interest in the meantime on dates spelled out in the bond contract.

Companies also have the option to issue equity securities such as common shares. When you invest in common stock, you are buying an ownership stake in the firm. You become a part owner and share in the company's fortunes, for better or for worse. Governments obviously cannot be owned, so they don't issue equity securities.

When you buy common stock you become a part owner in the firm.

If you own common stock, your shares' value may increase if the company prospers. You may also get dividends. Dividends are a share of company profits, paid to shareholders.

But if the company begins to do poorly, its share price may fall. It can even go to zero! And if the company goes under, shareholders' claims on the assets fall behind those of creditors, including bondholders. That's why stocks are generally considered riskier than bonds.

However, before a company can issue equity to the public, it has to become a corporation.

The role of the corporation

Basically, there are three types of business structures: sole proprietorships, partnerships and corporations. Corporations can often support larger and more complex organizations than can sole proprietorships and partnerships. On the flip side, proprietorships and partnerships are easier to set up and manage.

But proprietorships and partnerships also find it harder to expand by raising money. They typically rely on raising money by borrowing from banks or keeping profits from the business. However, large corporations have another option – they can issue securities like bonds and stocks.

They're able to do this since the corporation structure offers unique benefits. One is that the owners of the corporation have limited liability. That means they risk only the amount they have invested in the company's shares. In a sole proprietorship and a partnership, there is generally unlimited liability. The owners are personally liable to the business' creditors for any debts.

A corporation also offers continuity of existence. That means the company isn't necessarily wound up with the owner's death, as it is with a sole proprietorship, or with a partnership unless an agreement has been made to the contrary. When a shareholder of a corporation dies, the shares become part of the estate and are passed on to the heirs.

Another advantage of a corporation is that its shares or debt instruments are marketable. Shareholders of a public corporation can usually transfer their shares to other investors with relative ease. Being able to buy and sell shares of a corporation is an attractive feature for many investors.

How securities are traded

If you decide you want to buy art, you know you have to go to a gallery or an auction house. Those are actual, physical places where art is bought and sold. Securities, on the other hand, aren't quite as tangible as art. And the securities markets aren't always actual places.

In eighteenth-century Manhattan, Wall Street merchants sold stocks over the counter along with their regular merchandise. Stock markets with trading floors evolved from this primitive beginning. Nowadays, however, more and more trading floors are being closed, and stocks are being traded through networks of computers.

And even in the past, bonds usually weren't traded on floors, but over the telephone and via computer, as they continue to be today. Ironically enough, these computer and telephone-connected markets are called over-the-counter markets, reminiscent of the early days of Wall Street.

So a securities market isn't necessarily a physical place. Instead, it's the meeting place between orders to buy securities and orders to sell them. The bond market, for example, is basically the sum of all the orders to buy and sell bonds at any moment in time.

The markets are generally organized and operated by securities firms, such as stockbrokers and investment dealers. When a corporation issues new bonds and stocks to raise capital, investment dealers usually buy them and then resell them to the public. The initial sale from corporation to investment dealer takes place in what is known as the *primary market*.

The bond market is the sum of all the orders to buy and sell bonds at any moment in time.

Later, securities firms help facilitate the buying and selling of stocks and bonds already issued and outstanding. This is called the secondary market. There are secondary markets for both bonds and stocks, and they are what we generally think of when we refer to the bond market or the stock market.

Even when a market does exist physically – like the trading floors still found on some stock exchanges – you can't just go there and buy and sell stock. You have to make your trades through intermediary brokerages or investment dealers.

What Securities Dealers Do

In this day and age of instant global communication, you might be wondering why you have to go through a middleman in the first place. And why you have to pay a commission to a broker when you can trade from home over a PC.

The answer is easier to appreciate if you understand everything that happens behind the scenes after you place your buy or sell order. Say you own some stock in Abacus Inc. and you want to sell it. If you had to go to a trading floor, that would take time. And when you got there, you'd have to find someone willing to buy it from you. You'd have to negotiate the price. And to settle the trade, you'd have to hand over the certificate, and be paid by the buyer. Then you'd have to hope the buyer's cheque didn't bounce.

Your brokerage takes care of all of that for you. It ensures the trade takes place quickly, fairly, and at the best price possible at the time. It also makes sure that the buyer gets the securities they paid for, and that the seller gets paid. Many thousands of securities trades happen in Canada each day. This couldn't happen efficiently without experienced and trained personnel both at brokerage firms and other industry organizations.

You'll notice we've been using the phrase "brokerage firms" to describe the people who execute your orders to buy and sell securities. They are also referred to as securities firms, investment dealers, stockbrokers, and investment or brokerage houses.

At one time these terms meant different things. Investment dealers specialized in trading bonds, while brokerage firms focused on trading stocks. The terms also referred to the difference in how they traded them. Investment dealers that traded bonds generally acted as principals, while brokers trading stock acted as agents.

The brokerage as principal or agent

When a firm acts as a dealer or principal, it owns the securities at some point in the transaction. If you call an investment dealer and sell a bond, the dealer buys it from you with its own money. Afterwards, the dealer will resell your bond to another investor. The difference between what the dealer pays you for the bond and what it gets from the other investor is its profit or loss on the trade.

In contrast, when a broker acts as an agent, it brings together two investors who buy and sell from each other. The firm never owns the securities, and is paid a commission for its efforts in arranging the trade.

That's how the terms originated, but the distinctions between them have blurred over time. Now, most big securities firms trade both stocks and bonds. And they may act either as a principal or an agent. So when we use the term brokerage firm or investment dealer in this book, we are referring to securities firms generally unless we say otherwise. This isn't to suggest, however, that all securities firms do exactly the same type of work.

Types of brokerages

There's a large number of securities firms in Canada, and they differ from each other in many ways. Some have offices across the country, while others are focused on one region. Some have thousands of staff, others are "boutique" operations with just a few employees. Some offer an entire range of services, others focus on just a few areas. A firm's specialties might be trading securities in a particular industry; dealing only with a certain type of client like large institutions; managing portfolios for wealthy individuals; bond or stock trading; unlisted stock trading; or the underwriting of companies in certain sectors.

Securities firms differ in who owns and runs them. Historically, Canada divided the financial services industry into four major groups, known as the four pillars. These were the banks, the trust companies, the insurance companies and the securities industry. The government barred companies in one pillar from owning those in another pillar.

Today, the major banks in Canada own the largest securities firms.

This changed in mid-1987 when the government removed some of the cross-ownership barriers. This dramatically changed the shape of the securities industry. Today, the major banks in Canada own the largest securities firms, and there are many international players as well. But private or publicly traded independent companies remain a vibrant sector of the industry.

Securities firms also vary greatly in how they are structured. A big, integrated firm might have several departments, such as sales, underwriting, trading, research and administration. Sales staff deal with investors large or small. Underwriting specialists work on deals to raise capital for corporations or governments. Traders buy and sell stocks and bonds and other securities on behalf of the firm and its clients. The research department's analysts gather information on companies and issue reports on whether or not they are good buys. And administration covers all the various support functions, such as human resources, finance, compliance, and so on.

Underwriting new issues and IPOs

Underwriting is done when an investment dealer, acting as the underwriter, helps a company or government raise money by issuing new securities. The underwriting process may vary depending on whether the security involved is equity, corporate debt or government debt.

Perhaps the longest and most complicated process is when a company is making its first issue of stock to the public in an Initial Public Offering (IPO). A firm coming to market for the first time must file a preliminary prospectus with the provincial securities commission. A prospectus is a legal document that describes the securities being offered and it must be prepared in strict accordance with provincial securities law.

The prospectus

The prospectus should contain full, true and plain disclosure of all important facts about the issue. It should give you details about the underwriting and distribution; explain the company's history and its operations; highlight the risks of buying the securities; and include financial statements for the company.

When a firm files a preliminary prospectus, the provincial securities regulator reviews the preliminary prospectus and comments on any gaps in the information presented. Even when the regulator accepts the preliminary prospectus, it might not include the final price at which the securities will be offered to the public.

This is because the final price depends on investor demand. The underwriters and company managers will market the securities to investors in private meetings and group presentations in many cities or even several countries. The dealer's retail sales department may also offer the issue to suitable private clients, although the bulk of most issues are placed with institutions. The investment firms underwriting the offering advise the company on such matters as the price and size of the offering, based on their experience and on information the firms gather during a marketing period before the final prospectus is issued.

Once the underwriters get firm orders for the securities, the company then files a final prospectus with the regulators. This includes the price and size of the offering. If the regulator accepts the prospectus for filing, the offering can proceed.

It's critical to remember that by accepting the prospectus for filing, the regulator isn't saying that the securities are a good investment. It is merely saying that the prospectus meets its requirements for disclosing information about the securities.

By accepting the prospectus for filing, the regulator isn't saying the securities are a good investment.

After the final prospectus is filed, the investment firms in the underwriting group buy the securities from the company. The company pockets the money, and goes on its way. It's then up to the underwriters to sell the issue of securities to investors. Depending on the issue's size, the underwriting group may consist of anywhere from two to eight or nine investment firms. The bigger the issue, the more likely it is that multiple underwriters will be involved to reduce the risk exposure to any single firm. The underwriting group may also sell part of the issue to other securities firms, known as the Selling Group. This relieves the underwriters from having to sell the entire issue by themselves.

The process just described is a traditional, fully-marketed, long-form version of underwriting that can take several months. It's most often used for Initial Public Offerings and for subsequent equity or debt issues of companies that aren't large or well known.

Short-form offerings

To speed up the traditional underwriting process, the Canadian securities industry has developed a faster form of underwriting called the Prompt Offering Qualification System (POP). It's used for companies that are known in the market and that meet strict rules for continuous disclosure of material facts. In these cases, companies may not have to prepare a full prospectus because much of the information it would include is already available and widely known.

In a short-form offering, the company and the underwriters skip the lengthy process of issuing a preliminary prospectus and determining through investor road shows the best price for the issue. Instead, one or more securities firms will quickly make a deal with the company to buy the securities issue at an agreed upon price.

The underwriters then resell the securities to investors, bearing the risk that there might not be great interest in the issue or that market conditions might change, leaving them with an overpriced issue to sell. This is sometimes referred to as a "bought deal" underwriting. Often there will be no selling group involved in the bought deal process, so the underwriting group bears the risk alone.

Buying new issues

All of this might sound complicated, but from your point of view, you need to know only a few things.

First, remember that there may be more risk in stock of companies going public for the first time. This is partly because there is no past track record to judge the company by. As well, businesses often launch their IPOs when their industries are in fashion with investors. This lets them get a better price for their stock. However, you might be buying the stock at unusually high prices and just ahead of the industry falling out of favour.

Companies often launch their IPOs when their industries are in fashion.

If your investment advisor offers you the chance to buy some stock that's just being issued, ask what role your advisor's firm is playing in the underwriting. It may be that your broker has a quota of stock to sell, and you're being called because few other clients are interested. This is especially so if you usually aren't offered a chance to buy stock in an IPO. Even if your advisor calls you often about new offerings, you must by law be given a copy of the prospectus. Read it carefully and discuss any concerns with your advisor. As a rule, never agree to buy stock until you've read the prospectus.

During a distribution, you can by law withdraw from the agreement to buy the securities within two business days after getting or being considered to have received the prospectus. Most provinces also give you the right to rescind or cancel a contract if the prospectus contains false information. However, depending on the province you're in, you may have to choose between rescinding the contract or going to court to seek damages. Speak to a lawyer if you find yourself in this rare situation.

Trading in the Secondary Market

Let's say you own corporate bonds you bought in a new offering.

Now you decide you want to sell them. This is where the second key function of the securities dealer comes in – trading in the secondary market.

Bond trading

Bonds are typically traded in and out of a securities firm's own inventory, or from the inventory of other dealers that specialize in the issue. Your investment advisor will act as a principal in the trade, buying your bonds and then reselling them later to another firm or investor.

Most bond trading happens in the over-the-counter market.

The investment firm doesn't charge you commission on the trade. Instead they try to resell your bonds at a small profit. If you call your investment advisor and want to buy a bond, the dealer sells it to you out of its inventory. If it doesn't have the bond in inventory, the dealer will buy it from another firm and resell it to you.

Most bond trading takes place in the over-the-counter market via telephone and computer. The bond market is essentially a giant network of dealers and institutions. The only exceptions are a few corporate bonds that trade alongside the firm's stock on an exchange.

Stock trading

Most stock trading happens on an exchange – whether it's a virtual setting in cyberspace or a physical trading floor. An exchange is a central marketplace where buy and sell orders meet. When you call your broker to buy a stock, the firm usually sends your order to the exchange, where it's matched with a sell order. The exchanges have rules and systems in place to ensure that orders are executed as quickly as possible, and at the best possible price.

Occasionally your order might be matched with one from another of the firm's clients. Called a "cross" transaction, this mostly happens at large firms with thousands of clients trading daily. Even if the order is matched internally, the trade is considered an agency trade and details are immediately reported to the relevant exchange.

If you think about it, together the brokerage firms are the market. This is obvious for the over-the-counter markets with their networks of brokers. But it's also true for stock exchanges. Although exchanges are often mistaken for government bodies, a stock exchange is traditionally owned by a group of investment dealers. Dealers that belong to a certain exchange are known as member firms. However, even the ownership structure of exchanged is changing. Several exchanges around the world, including the Toronto Stock Exchange, are moving to become publicly-traded companies themselves.

Canada has two major stock exchanges. The biggest is the Toronto Stock Exchange (TSE), which is the country's senior stock market. It's where most large company stocks trade. Most small company shares trade on the Canadian Venture Exchange (CDNX). Both of these markets have closed their trading floors in favour of computerized systems. In addition to the two big exchanges, a limited number of small company shares are listed on the Montreal Exchange.

Regulating the securities markets

Integrity is obviously essential to the success of Canada's capital markets. If investors are to participate, then there must be some assurance that they will be dealing on a level playing field.

The Canadian securities system is generally well regulated and efficient. Of course, no system can completely insulate itself from problems. Complex checks and balances are in place to help ensure honesty and fairness in the markets, but these aren't foolproof. That's why you need to know how the system works so that you can be vigilant against potential problems.

The securities commissions

Ultimate authority over the country's securities industry lies in the hands of the provincial securities administrators, often known as securities commissions. They possess wide powers under provincial laws called securities acts.

The general principle of Canada's securities laws isn't approving or rejecting the merits of an issue of securities offered for sale. Just because a security can be sold in a province, doesn't mean the securities administrator believes it is a worthy investment.

Instead, the administrators try to ensure that those offering securities provide you with full, true and plain disclosure of all relevant facts. This is usually done in a prospectus, and after that in ongoing updates like annual reports and annual information forms.

Investment firms and their representatives must register with their provincial securities commission.

In addition, investment firms and their representatives have to be registered with the securities commission in the province where they work or where they sell securities. To become registered, individuals must meet minimum industry education requirements. They may also need to have a certain amount of previous experience. The requirements vary depending on the type of work the person does.

The commissions also have the power to suspend or cancel registrations of individuals or investment firms to protect the public interest. They can investigate, undertake prosecutions for violations of the acts, conduct hearings, take evidence under oath, seize documents for examination, freeze funds or securities and impose settlement penalties.

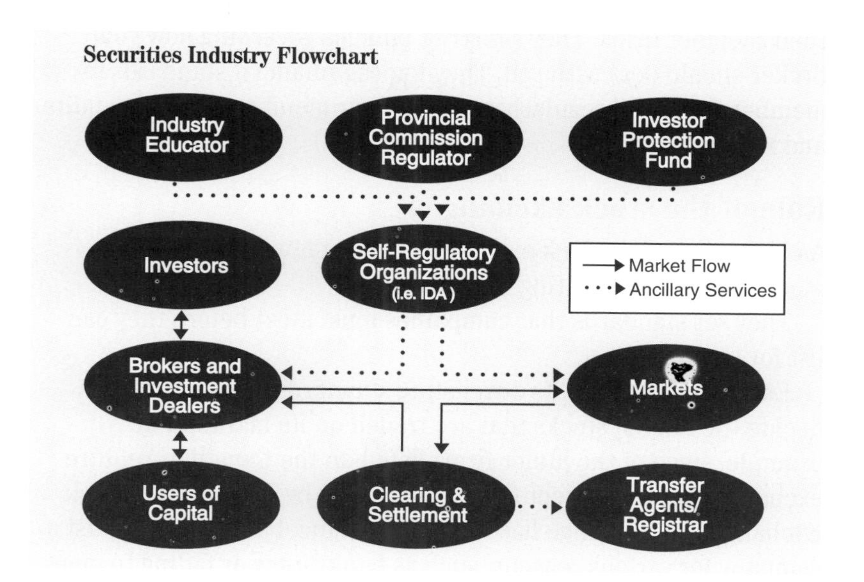

Although the commissions can't force a company or individual to pay money back to an investor, they can halt trading in a security and deny the right to trade securities in the province. They may also recommend that a charge be laid in the courts should they find that a section of the Securities Act has been violated. That charge might result in a guilty party being fined or imprisoned or both.

Unlike in the United States, there is no federal regulatory body in Canada. While the national Securities and Exchange Commission (SEC) monitors the capital markets south of the border, the Canadian equivalents are the provincial securities administrators. However, to ensure there's some continuity between the provinces, each provincial commission belongs to an umbrella organization called the Canadian Securities Administrators (CSA). Members of the CSA work together to ensure that provincial securities regulations are similar across the country.

However, while ultimate authority rests with the securities administrators, the industry itself does much of the day-to-day regulation. It does this through organizations like the IDA and the Montreal Exchange that have status as Self-Regulatory Organizations (SROs). The SROs' rules cover a wide range of areas. They enforce education and training standards for employees of their member firms. They set strict policies governing how your broker should deal with you. They impose financial standards for member firms and regularly monitor their members through audits and reports.

Role of the stock exchanges

As SROs, Canada's stock exchanges play an important role in monitoring and regulating the markets.

They set standards that companies must meet before they can list for trading.

Each exchange has its own listing standards, and these help decide the kind of stocks that are traded on its market. For example, some of the junior firms listed on the Canadian Venture exchange might not meet the standards set by The Toronto Stock Exchange. An exchange has the right to cancel a listing or de-list a company for various reasons, such as bankruptcy or failing to meet the exchange's listing standards.

Each exchange is also responsible for regulating its market and checking that traders and other market participants follow the exchange's trading rules. Major exchanges also devote considerable resources to market surveillance – watching market activity to detect any unusual price or volume changes in stocks. Detecting unusual changes is important because it may indicate improper activity such as illegal insider trading. If the exchanges suspect a rule has been violated, they will follow-up with an investigation.

While Canada's stock exchanges have different standards and rules, they try to coordinate the rules for their member dealers, many of which belong to more than one exchange.

The Investment Dealers Association

Just like the stock exchanges monitor their markets, the Investment Dealers Association of Canada monitors the bond and money markets. As an SRO, the IDA regulates its member securities firms, many of which also are members of an exchange.

Now, you could be forgiven for thinking that the idea of an SRO is a bit like asking the fox to guard the hen house. But there are solid reasons why it's a good idea for the industry to police itself. First of all, as you can imagine, people in the industry are far more knowledgeable about the securities business than anyone outside it. People who know the markets are better able to spot potential problems and make effective rules. As well, self-regulation means the industry bears the high cost of setting rules and enforcing compliance with them.

Also, it's wrong to imagine that the industry can do anything it wants with no regard for public interest. Look at the diagram on page 13 showing how the securities industry works. At the top and centre of the diagram is a box for the provincial commission regulators.

So far, we've only talked about the role of SROs and the regulators within the securities industry. However, as the diagram on page 13 indicates, there are several other important players involved in maintaining a fair, efficient and vibrant market. For example, the box on the top left is marked Industry Educator. This is the Canadian Securities Institute, publisher of this book.

How and Why the CSI Evolved

Over the years, the main Canadian exchanges and the Investment Dealers Association recognized that they share several common functions. For example, all of them employ staff who need to be educated about securities. So they decided to jointly sponsor an organization to look after the education of brokers, other members of the industry and the public at large. This is the role of the Canadian Securities Institute.

Canadian Investor Protection Fund

There are a few other organizations that the SROs, and the investment dealers who are their members, sponsor together. An important one is the Canadian Investor Protection Fund, or CIPF. You may have heard about this under its previous name, the National Contingency Fund.

The CIPE offers you protection if your brokerage goes insolvent.

This fund helps protect you in case your brokerage firm goes under. It works in a similar way to the deposit insurance for banks that many of you probably know about. The CIPF covers losses in a customer's general account of up to $1,000,000 in cash and securities. Say, for example, that you had $50,000 in cash in your account and $250,000 in stocks and bonds. Even if your brokerage firm went under and was unable to pay you back, all of this would be protected by the industry fund, for a total of $300,000. So you wouldn't lose a dime.

Remember, though, that the CIPF is intended to protect people in case a brokerage firm fails financially. It does not protect you from normal losses in the market. For example, if you invested $100,000 in the stock of Mosquito Farms Inc., and it went bankrupt and the stock plummeted to zero, you might well lose all of your investment. This fund doesn't protect you from making investment decisions that turn out badly. It only protects you in case the brokerage firm which holds your account and your securities goes under.

It's also important to note that the Canadian Investor Protection Fund only protects you if your account is with a member of one of the fund's sponsors. These are the Toronto Stock Exchange and the Canadian Venture Exchange, the Montreal Exchange and the Investment Dealers Association of Canada. If your brokerage is a member of one of these organizations, your accounts are protected. But not all brokerages are members of the IDA or one of these exchanges. So keep this in mind when you start looking for a broker.

The Role of the Clearing House

There's another vital industry organization you should know about. It's the clearing corporation. When a trade takes place, there's a buyer and a seller. The buyer has to pay for the stock, and the seller has to supply the certificate proving ownership of the stock. And this happens thousands of times a day on the markets.

To keep track of it all, we have a clearing corporation, sometimes called a depository. In Canada, there is one national clearing corporation, for debt and equity securities. The Canadian Depository for Securities Limited (CDS). It's used by members of the IDA, the TSE, the Montreal Exchange, the Canadian Venture Exchange, as well as some banks and trust companies.

The clearing corporation's work is quite complex. Computers are used extensively to keep track of all the purchases and sales of securities. As an investor, you need to know that you generally have three business days to settle up when you buy or sell stocks and some bonds. Traditionally, that has meant you have three days to pay for a purchase, and three days to turn in your securities certificates if you are selling.

Street Name Registration

Today, most people who own stocks don't actually hold the stock certificates. Instead, they likely have their securities registered with a broker. This option, otherwise known as holding your certificates in "street name", enables you to avoid the hassle of finding somewhere to keep certificates safe as well as making sure they get to your broker quickly when its time to sell them.

Actually, your broker probably doesn't hold the certificates either because the industry has moved rapidly toward paperless settlement in the past few years. In most cases, when a security is transferred from one brokerage firm to another, the certificate doesn't actually move. What moves is an entry in a book showing who owns the stock. And who owes money to pay for the stock.

At the end of each trading day, transactions between investment dealers are added up for every security. So if an investor who deals with investment dealer A bought a stock from an investor at dealer B, the clearing corporation sends a tab to dealer A to pay for the stock, and changes the entry in the book to show that dealer B no longer holds that stock. The process is similar for bond transactions.

It all sounds complicated, and given the number of trades that happen each day, it's pretty impressive. But it's the fastest, safest way to make sure you get paid when you sell a security, and get ownership of a security when you pay for it.

Of course, certificates are still issued for various reasons, including the fact that some people just feel more secure about their investment if they can hold proof of it in their hands. The fact is, however, that even without the certificate you do have proof that you own the stock. The proof is in your account statements. And second, think of it as if you were depositing money in the bank. You probably don't keep cash stuffed in your mattress. What you have is a bank statement showing that you have a certain amount of cash in the bank. The bank keeps that cash a lot safer than you could. And it's the same with stocks. Most investors choose not to worry about the certificates getting lost or stolen when the broker will do that for them.

The Transfer Agent

If you refer once more to the diagram on page 13, you'll notice that there's one more box we haven't covered yet. It contains transfer agents and registrars and it has direct links to the clearing and settlement function.

Unlike the other organizations, these are not industry-sponsored groups. A transfer agent is a trust company appointed by a corporation to keep track of its shareholders. The agent records who the shareholders are and where they live. A list of shareholders is important so that shareholders get any dividends they are entitled to and are notified about meetings where they may be eligible to vote, such as the annual meeting. The registrar double-checks the transfer agent's work and keeps tabs on the status of a firm's shares.

What's in it for you?

Basically, there are two ways you can earn a return on an investment. First, you can get growth of your capital. That means your investment can rise in value. If you're looking for capital growth, you might buy a common stock in a firm you think has good growth prospects.

Second, you can make money by getting regular income on your investment. Income from a security might be the interest you make on a bond or the dividends you might get from shares you own.

Of course, many investments, such as shares in established or "blue chip" companies offer potential for both – capital growth through a gain in share price and regular income through dividends.

Besides capital growth and income, another investment objective to keep in mind is safety of principal. If an investment has guaranteed safety, you are sure to get back what you invested. However, if you are mostly seeking safety in an investment, then you may have to settle for less income and capital gains potential. Good examples in Canada are federal government debt instruments – such as bonds and treasury bills. They have a high degree of safety, so they generally offer you less of a return than higher risk investments like most corporate bonds and stocks. On the plus side, though, your return is virtually guaranteed.

Growth of your capital and regular income are the two key returns offered by investments.

The fourth major investment consideration is called liquidity. A security is liquid if you can buy or sell it on short notice, with little effect on the price. If you may need to get at your money quickly, you need a liquid investment. Money in most bank accounts is highly liquid. At the other end of the scale, real estate or art objects are often illiquid. If you need to sell them quickly, you might have to accept a lower price than if you were able to wait for a better offer.

If there was such a thing, the perfect security would meet all four objectives. It would offer a big increase in capital, lots of steady income, guaranteed safety of principal and the ability to be sold at a moment's notice. Unfortunately, there's no perfect security. When you buy a security, you are usually making a trade-off between these four objectives.

Which objectives you favour will depend on your financial situation and your goals. An elderly widow might need safety of principal and a regular income. A well-off young executive, meanwhile, might have the income and the daring to take bigger risks in the hopes of retiring early.

Making the Trade-Off Between Risk and Return

The most important rule in investing is also the simplest to understand. The greater the potential for making money in the capital markets, the greater your chances of losing money, too.

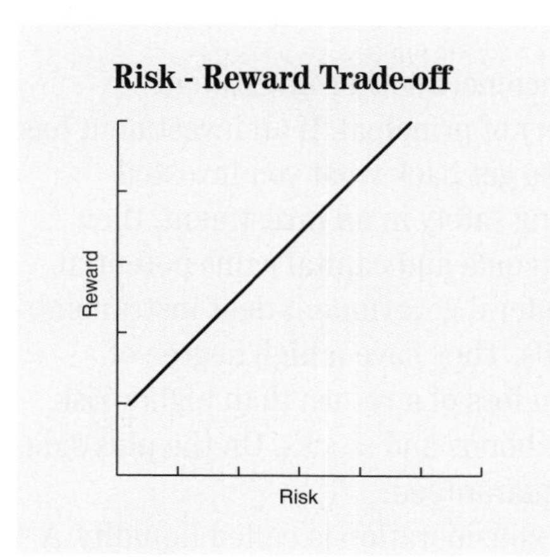

Every investment decision you make boils down to this inevitable trade-off. If a security promises above-average returns, it almost certainly harbors higher risks as well. Similarly, if you are willing to endure higher risks, then you want to be rewarded with higher returns. Learning how to balance the returns you want with the risks you are prepared to take is every investor's perpetual challenge.

There are some general rules of thumb you can use to assess risk levels in different investments:

- Debt securities like GICs and bonds are safer than ownership securities like stocks;
- Government securities are generally safer than corporate securities;
- The shorter the security's term, the safer it generally is;
- An investment that pays you income is typically safer than one that doesn't;
- Stocks of large, profitable companies are usually safer than those of smaller companies; and,
- Investments in developed countries are safer than those in less developed or emerging market nations.

But be warned, there's a great deal of variation within these categories. All government bonds, for example, are not created equal. Those issued by a large country like Canada are safer than bonds issued by a small emerging market country. In fact, some emerging market bonds may be riskier than some stocks.

If this sounds confusing, relax. In subsequent chapters, you'll learn how to analyze and compare the investment merits of different securities.

Summary

The investment markets are the meeting place for suppliers of capital, who have surplus funds to invest, and users, who have a need for extra money. Business and government users borrow money by issuing debt securities such as bonds and debentures. Businesses can also raise money by selling shares in themselves, otherwise known as equity. Financial intermediaries such as investment dealers facilitate the issuing and trading of these securities.

Suppliers choose their investments to satisfy their objectives, which may be capital growth, income or both. Safety of principal and liquidity of investment are also key considerations. Each of these has an impact on a given investment's risk and reward, which are closely related.

This chapter explains the more detailed workings of the securities markets. Investment dealers are one of the key players. Canadian investment dealers differ in terms of size and areas of specialization. A dealer can function either as a principal or as an agent. A principal owns the securities that it sells, whereas an agent acts as an intermediary between a buyer and seller. One of the dealers' major functions is to underwrite or bring to market new issues of securities. Once an issue has been sold, it will trade on the secondary market, either on an over-the-counter market or a stock exchange.

The Self Regulatory Organizations (SROs) are another major part of the securities system. These are the stock exchanges and the Investment Dealers Association. They create trading rules and monitor events. The provinces also regulate the markets through their securities commissions.

Other organizations that are part of the system are the Canadian Investor Protection Fund (CIPF), which protects investors against losses caused by the failure of a dealer; the clearing corporation such as CDS and the transfer agents and registrars, who keep track of a firm's shareholders.

There are two ways to make money as an investor: You can either loan your money, or become an owner.

Investing is balancing risk and return. Generally, the potential for higher returns comes from investments that carry higher risk.

Bonds, Debentures and the Money Market

When corporations and governments borrow money, that creates an opportunity for investors to earn a return.

Borrowing money is a key part of the capitalization process – it's one of the major sources of a company's capital structure. It's interesting to note that governments too are a part of this process. But whereas companies can also raise money by issuing equity, that is, by selling shares in themselves, governments cannot. Their money comes mostly from us, in the form of taxes, and from lenders, who may also be us, in the form of government debt instruments such as Canada Savings Bonds, treasury bills and bonds.

Instead of going to the bank, corporations often borrow from individuals or institutions with money to invest. They issue what is essentially an I.O.U., except they call it a bond, debenture, or sometimes other names. What it's called depends on how long it's for, what is going to guarantee that the borrowed money actually gets paid back, and the features, if any, that accompany it.

When you buy a bond or debenture you make a loan to the business enterprise or the government who issued it.

When you buy a bond or debenture you make a loan to the business enterprise or the government body that issued it. The issuer promises to pay this money back to you on the maturity date and in the meantime, to pay you interest at set amounts on regular and specified dates, usually semi-annually. Bonds and debentures are issued in Canada by the federal government, by the ten provinces, by municipalities, by government agencies, by business corporations and, occasionally, by religious organizations.

The Difference between Bonds and Debentures

Debt securities issued by municipalities are usually called debentures. Traditionally, a debenture is a debt security that is an unsecured promise to pay. In other words, there's no property or assets pledged as security for the loan.

This is precisely what a Government of Canada bond is, but custom has established that we speak of Government of Canada bonds, not debentures. Provincial issues may sometimes be designated as bonds and sometimes as debentures. However, securities issued by municipalities and corporate debt issues that are not specifically secured by certain assets are debentures, even though they are sometimes referred to as bonds.

Over the years, a great variety of bonds and debentures has been issued, but we will limit our discussion to the more important types of government and corporate money market instruments, bonds and debentures.

Finding the Right Bond

Knowing which type of bond best meets your investment objectives depends on knowing more about the choices available to you. Let's start by looking at some of the properties that make bonds similar or different from each other.

ACME Ltd. 8.00% bonds due September 1, 2004 pay $4.00 for every $100 face value on March 1 and September 1 of each year, with the final payment on September 1, 2004.

Bonds maturing:	Term:
up to three years	short term
from three to ten years	medium term
over ten years	long term

The Interest or Coupon Rate

Every bond states on its face the rate of interest that the bond carries. This rate is known as the coupon rate. Interest payments are usually made twice a year at six-month intervals and one of the payment dates is the same as the day and month of the maturity date.

Maturity Date

The maturity date is the date on which the amount borrowed is repayable and interest payments end. Bonds usually mature at any time from one to 30 years and sometimes longer. There is no set rule covering the term. However, depending on the time remaining to maturity, the informal guidelines you see here are used in the bond market.

Term to Maturity

The designation of the term of a bond or debenture depends on the time remaining to maturity, and a debt issue will change its term status as the maturity date approaches. For example, a bond issued in 2000 and due in 2020 was initially a long-term issue with a 20-year term to maturity. In 2010, the term to maturity will become ten years, so the same bond will then be considered medium term. In 2017, term to maturity will be three years and the issue will be considered short term.

Callable Bonds

Issuers of bonds often reserve the right to pay off the bond before maturity to take advantage of lower interest rates, or to use accumulated funds to eliminate interest charges. This privilege is known as the call feature or redemption feature and a bond bearing this clause is known as a callable bond or a redeemable bond. As a rule, the issuer agrees to give 30 days or more notice to the bondholder that the bond is being called or redeemed.

Debt that cannot be called before its maturity is known as non-callable or non-redeemable.

Denomination or Face Value

The amount the issuer of the bond contracts to pay on maturity is shown on the face of the bond. This is known as the denomination or face value. The most commonly used denominations are $1,000 or $10,000 and larger denominations to suit the preference of institutions such as banks and life insurance companies. Normally, an issue designed for a broad retail market is issued in small denominations. Compound interest Canada Savings Bonds, for example, are issued in denominations as low as $100. An issue designed for institutional investors, on the other hand, is made available in denominations reaching into millions of dollars to suit the needs of the buyer.

How to Classify Bonds

A bond is a debt instrument with a pledge of an asset behind it.

Generally, you can classify corporate bonds in two ways. One is to group bonds by how they are secured. Here we have such bond types as mortgage bonds, debentures and notes.

You can further classify bonds by the rights and privileges attached to them, such as those of redemption, conversion and sinking fund. Thus, we have redeemable bonds, sinking fund and purchase fund bonds, income bonds, extendible and retractable bonds, serial bonds and convertible bonds, to name a few.

Through various combinations of provisions for security and special features, a considerable number of different types of bonds have been brought into existence. You can find out the characteristics of any given bond by examining its title.

Generally, a bond is a debt instrument with a pledge of an asset behind it. If the issuer can't pay the interest or return the principal at maturity, the lenders have a claim on that asset. A debenture, on the other hand, is a debt issue without a physical asset pledged as collateral.

A debenture is a debt issue without a physical asset pledged as collaterial.

Just to make things a little more confusing, the term bonds is commonly used to refer to any debt issue, regardless of its security. Government of Canada bonds, for example, really aren't bonds because there's no asset behind them. They are debentures, but we use the broader term bonds to refer to them. Keep in mind, though, that the government's powers of taxation can function as a type of security for its debt issues.

Some of the most common forms of bonds and debentures are described below.

Mortgage Bonds

As most Canadian homeowners know, a mortgage is a legal

document containing an agreement to pledge land, buildings, or equipment as security for a loan. It entitles the lender to take over ownership of these properties if you fail to pay interest or repay principal when due. The mortgage is held by the lender until the loan is repaid and is then cancelled or destroyed. It's not exercised unless you fail to satisfy the terms of the loan.

There is no fundamental difference between a mortgage and a mortgage bond except in form. Both are issued to secure property to the lender in the event of failure to repay a loan.

Since it's impractical for a corporation to issue separate mortgages securing portions of its properties to each lender, the same result is achieved by issuing one mortgage on its properties. The mortgage is then deposited with a trustee, usually a trust company, which acts for all lenders or investors in safeguarding their interests under the terms of the loan contract described in the mortgage. The amount of the loan is divided into convenient portions, usually $1,000, or multiples of $1,000, and each investor gets a bond as evidence of his proportionate participation in the loan to the firm and the claim under the terms of the mortgage. This instrument is a mortgage bond.

First Mortgage Bonds

First mortgage bonds are the most senior securities a firm can offer because they form a first claim on the company's assets, earnings and undertakings before unsecured current liabilities are paid. Prospective investors should study each first mortgage issue to find out exactly what properties are covered by the mortgage. Most Canadian first mortgage bonds carry a first and specific charge against the firm's fixed assets and a floating charge on all other assets. They are generally regarded as the best security a company can issue, particularly if the mortgage applies to all fixed assets of the firm owned now and those acquired later. This last phrase is called the after acquired clause.

Collateral Trust Bonds

A collateral trust bond is one that is secured, not by a pledge of property as in a mortgage bond, but by physical pledge of other securities.

To provide a greater measure of security for a mortgage bond, collateral in the form of bonds and stocks may also be pledged. Such bonds are called mortgage and collateral trust bonds. First mortgage and collateral trust bonds are secured by first mortgage and by the deposit with the trustee of other corporate securities such as bonds or shares of subsidiaries.

Debentures

A debenture in simple terms is an unsecured bond. It's a direct obligation, or a promise to pay, of the issuing company, but it does not have a specific claim or assignment on assets or property. A debenture ranks behind current liabilities, if so specified, and/or first and general mortgage bonds. In effect, the security is the general credit of the issuer. Sometimes, they are partly secured by certain assets that are not sufficient to provide a full mortgage, such as the assets of a subsidiary or a regional operation. In such cases they are known as secured debentures.

Corporate Debentures

Corporations issue debentures for several reasons. One is that the nature of the business may be commercial or mercantile and there are few assets that can be pledged under a mortgage. Another is that the fixed assets have already been pledged under a closed mortgage that does not permit the issuance of further bonds. In other cases, it may not be possible to establish clear title to some land and buildings. Finally, some corporations are so well known and highly regarded that they can borrow from investors on favorable terms without having to pledge any company assets.

Subordinated Debentures

Subordinated debentures are debentures that are junior to another security issued by the company or another debt assumed by the firm. This means that holders of subordinated debentures will stand in line behind regular debenture holders if an issuer has trouble paying its debts.

Corporate Notes

A corporate note is simply an unsecured promise made by the borrower to pay interest and repay the funds borrowed at a specific date or dates. Corporate notes rank behind all other fixed interest securities of the borrower.

Finance companies often use a type of note called a secured note or a collateral trust note. When you buy a car on credit, you make a cash down payment and sign a series of notes agreeing to make more payments on specified dates. The automobile dealer takes these notes to a finance company, which discounts them and pays the dealer in cash. Finance companies pledge notes like these as security for collateral trust notes. These notes are of various maturities and are sold to individual investors with substantial portfolios as well as to financial institutions.

Debt Classified by Feature

Now let's look at some of the features that a bond might have. We've already talked about extendibles and retractables, but there are others.

Redeemable (or Callable) Bonds and Debentures

Corporate bond or debenture issues usually have a call feature, which is used at the corporation's option. The call price is usually set above the par value of the bond to compensate the holder for the loss of coupon income that will result from the redemption. The closer the bond is to its maturity date before it's redeemed, the less is the hardship to the investor. The redemption price is therefore often on a graduated scale and the premium payment becomes less as the bond draws closer to maturity. Debt that cannot be called prior to maturity is known as non-callable or non-redeemable.

Sinking Fund and Purchase Fund Bonds and Debentures

Sinking funds are sums of money set aside out of earnings each year to provide for the repayment of all or part of a debt issue by maturity. Most corporate debt issues carry a sinking fund provision, which is as binding on the issuer as any mortgage provision. A debt issue that carries a sinking fund arrangement usually indicates this in its title.

The sinking fund is a convenience to the issuer as some of the issue is paid off earlier than the maturity date, thus lessening the cash drain when eventual maturity is reached. It's not really a convenience for the holder since it may result in your bonds being called, even though you may have been planning to hold them till maturity.

Some companies prefer a purchase fund over a sinking fund. A purchase fund is set up to retire a specified amount of the outstanding bonds and debentures through purchases in the market, provided such purchases can be made at or below a stipulated price.

The purchase fund normally retires less of an issue than a sinking fund. Also, there are no provisions for calling bonds as in the case of a sinking fund, and there's normally fewer mandatory features.

Occasionally, a firm will have a sinking fund and a purchase fund together.

Convertible Bonds and Debentures

Convertible debentures combine certain advantages of a bond with the option of exchanging the bond for common shares. In effect, a convertible bond gives you a play on the common shares of the company.

Convertible debentures or bonds possess a special right to be exchanged into common shares on specifically determined terms called the conversion privilege. They possess the characteristics of bonds and debentures because they carry a fixed interest rate and a definite maturity date. They also offer the possibility of greater capital appreciation than regular bonds through the right to convert them into common shares at stated prices over stated periods.

A convertible bond gives you a play on the common shares of the company.

Why Convertible are Issued

The addition of a conversion privilege makes a debenture more saleable. It tends to lower the cost of the money borrowed and may enable the firm to raise equity capital indirectly on terms more favorable than through the sale of common shares.

The convertible has also been used to interest investors in providing capital for companies when they would not have been interested in buying low-yielding or non-dividend paying common shares.

The convertible debenture is a two-way security – one that combines much of the safety and certainty of income of the bond with the option of converting it into common shares if and when the investor sees a promising opportunity for capital appreciation. The convertible has a special appeal for the investor who wants to share in the firm's growth but wishes to avoid any substantial risk and is willing to accept the lower yield of the convertible to profit from growth in the common shares.

Characteristics of Convertibles

In most convertible debentures, the conversion price is graduated upward over the years to encourage early conversion. In view of the ability of most Canadian companies to grow in net worth and earning capacity, this arrangement would seem to be reasonable.

Convertible debentures may normally be converted into stock at any time up until the conversion privilege expires. They are normally callable – usually at a small premium and after reasonable notice.

Convertible debentures may be converted into stock at any time up until the conversion privilege expires.

The Forced Conversion Clause

This clause is built into some convertible debt issues to give the issuing firm more scope in calling in the debt for redemption under certain circumstances. Such a redemption provision usually states that once the market price of the common stock is higher than a specified level for a specific number of days, the firm can call the bonds for redemption at a stipulated price. The price, of course, would be much lower than the level at which the convertible debt would be trading because of the rise in the price of the common stock. Holders would choose to convert rather than have their debt called away at the lower redemption price.

This provision is an advantage to the issuing company rather than to the debt holder. The forced conversion can improve the firm's debt-equity ratio and enable new debt financing to take place. However, it's not onerous to the debt holder to the point of detracting from an issue when it's first sold.

Choosing the Right Convertible Debenture

With all these different features, it can be difficult to choose the type of convertible debenture that's right for you, not to mention the best time to buy it. There are, however, a few basic rules that can make your decision easier:

- try to get the highest quality debenture you can;
- buy it as close as possible to the price it would be worth if it had no conversion privilege;
- look for a conversion privilege that is realistic in terms of your estimate of the firm's future growth;
- buy the convertible when stock prices are depressed, if the convertible is at a discount. There is no point in buying a convertible if the conversion prices are above not only the present price but the prices at which you estimate the shares will sell in the years covered by the privilege.

Market Performance of Convertibles

Market prices of convertible debentures are influenced by their investment value and by the price level of the underlying common shares. Generally, their prices rise along with increases in the prices of the common shares, and decline in value when the common stock price falls, but only to the levels at which they represent competitive values as straight debenture investments.

Convertible debentures tend to behave as follows. When the stock of the issuing company is well below the conversion price, the convertible debenture acts like a straight debenture, responding to the general level of interest rates, the activity of the sinking fund and the quality of the security.

When the stock approaches the conversion price, a premium appears. For example, a $1,000 debenture might be convertible into 40 shares of stock ($25 per share). This convertible would sell somewhat above $1,000, perhaps at $1,100. This premium reflects the desires of investors to hold a two-way security. Although what forms a reasonable premium varies, 15% to 20% or lower is often considered attractive.

When the common stock rises above the conversion price, the debenture will rise in price accordingly and is then said to be selling off the stock. If in our example the common stock rises to $30 per share, the price of the convertible debenture will rise to 40 times $30, or $1,200, plus some premium.

Pay-back Period

The pay-back period on a convertible debenture is a key evaluation tool for these securities. Pay-back period is the time it takes the convertible to recoup its premium through its higher yield, compared with the dividend that is paid on the stock. Pay-back periods of two years or less are usually considered attractive.

Floating Rate Debentures

Floating rate debentures have proved popular because of the protection they offer to investors during periods of volatile interest rates. When interest rates are moving up, the interest paid is adjusted upward, with a resultant beneficial effect on the price and yield of the debentures. The disadvantage to these debentures is evident when their interest payable moves down as a result of a drop in rates. The minimum rate on the debentures can provide some protection to this process, though it's normally quite low.

Calculating Bond Yields

While tax implications are important, most people are probably more concerned with the pre-tax return on their investments. In the case of bonds, that means knowing how to work out what's known as the bond's yield. Let's start with a couple of definitions.

A $10,000 bond that you buy for $10,000, plus accrued interest, is said to have been bought at par. A bond that you buy for less than par is said to have been bought at a discount, while a bond you buy for more than par is said to have been bought at a premium.

Yield to the investment industry is the annual income from an investment expressed as a percentage of the cost or market price. In the case of stocks, yield is simply the indicated annual dividend expressed as a percentage of the market price. But with most bonds, this relationship is complicated by the assumption that you'll be repaid the par value of your investment at maturity.

Yields Include Interest and Capital Gains

Unlike a stock yield, a bond yield not only reflects your return in the form of income, but also makes allowance for any capital gain or loss realized when the bond matures. So, a bond yield to maturity is made up partly of income and partly of capital gain or loss.

Suppose, for example, that you bought at par an 8% $5,000 bond maturing in six years. If you held it to maturity, you would get $400 each year in interest (8% of $5,000) and your capital gain or loss is $0. The reason is that the bond was bought at par and will be paid off at par on maturity, so no gain or loss results. The gross or pre-tax return would then be:

$$\frac{\$8 \text{ (income)}}{\$100 \text{ (purchase price)}} = 8\%$$

Now you might be wondering why we are using these numbers. Did we not just say that the income is $400, not $8? Yes, we did. But when it comes to yield calculations, the industry always expresses it in terms of one year and for $100 face value. Thus, whatever income you earn for each $100 of face value is the numerator. And the amount you paid for each $100 of face value is the denominator. In this case, $8 divided by $100 results in a yield of 8%.

Purchasing Bonds at other Than Par Value

That may seem simple, but it gets more complicated when you buy bonds for more or less than their par value. Suppose, for example, the same 8% $5,000 bond was bought at a discount, say for $94. (This might occur if interest rates were to rise subsequent to the bond's issue, thus making its promised rate of interest less attractive). The income received per $100 face value is the same: $8. We also have to consider the capital gain which in this case is a straightforward $6.

However, since we're looking at the income received in one year, we should do the same for the capital gain. Six dollars over a six-year period is $1 per annum. In this case your annual pre-tax return is:

$ 8	**income**
$ 1	**capital gain**
$ 9	**total**

So, the pre-tax yield is: $\frac{\$9}{\$94} = 9.57\%$

In practice, it has been found that an answer close to the correct answer can be obtained by using the average of the purchase price and redemption price at maturity as the divisor.

For example:

$$\frac{94 + 100}{2} = 97$$

and: $$\frac{9}{97} = 9.28\%$$

Not surprisingly, this type of yield calculation is called the average purchase/redemption price or rough yield calculation.

Reading Bond Quotations

One of first steps in considering a bond investment is finding out about its price. To do that, you simply need to refer to the bond quote section of your newspaper. It will look something like this:

Issue	Coupon rate	Maturity	Bid	Ask
ABC Company	6.26%	5 Aug./04	98.61	99.11

This quotation would mean that, at the time reported, a 6.26% coupon bond or debenture of ABC Company which matures on August 5, 2004 could be sold for $986.10 and bought at $991.10 per $1,000 face or principal amount. Some financial newspapers publish a single price for the bond or debenture, which may be the bid price, the midpoint between the final bid and ask quote for the day, or a price which is an estimate at current interest rate levels. Convertible issues are usually marked by an asterisk or grouped together separately.

Extendible and Retractable Bonds

Extendibles

Extendible bonds and debentures are usually issued with a short maturity term but with the option for the holder to extend the debt for an additional term at the same or slightly higher rate of interest. In effect, the extendible bondholder can extend the maturity of the bond from short to mid or long term.

If the ABC Company debenture were extendible it would usually appear in the financial pages as follows:

Issue	Coupon rate	Maturity	Bid	Ask
ABC Company	6.26%	5 Aug. 04/09	98.61	99.11

The holder of this debenture would have the option of extending the term of the debenture from August 5, 2004 to August 5, 2009.

Retractables

Retractable bonds are the opposite to extendible bonds. They are issued with a long maturity term but with the option for the holder to turn in the bond for redemption at par several years sooner. In effect, the retractable bondholder can retract or pull back the maturity of the bond from a long to a shorter-term date.

If the ABC Company debenture were retractable, it would usually appear in the financial pages in the following way:

Issue	Coupon rate	Maturity	Bid	Ask
ABC Company	6.26%	5 Aug.09/04	99.25	99.75

The holder of this bond is able to redeem the bond on August 5, 2004 instead of holding it to August 5, 2009.

Built-in Flexibility

Buyers are attracted by the flexibility of extendible and retractable issues, and as a result they sell at a lower yield than straight issues. One of the factors you must consider when choosing a bond term is where you think interest rates are going. If you think they are going up, you would choose a short-term bond so as not to get stuck with today's issue when the ones coming out next year will have more

Extendible and retractable issues are referred to as variable maturity or exchange-able debt.

attractive rates. If you think interest rates are headed down, you would want a longer-term bond, to lock in today's higher rates. Extendibles and retractables let you hedge your bets; you can decide later on the term.

You make your decision during the election period, which normally lasts for six months. The election period normally occurs from one year to six months before the first maturity date. With extendibles, you use this period to notify the appropriate trustee or agent of the debt issuer whether you wish to extend the term of the bond or allow it to mature on the earlier date. If you take no action, the bond automatically matures on the earlier date. With retractables, you must take action if you want to exercise the retraction option during this period; if you do nothing, the debt automatically remains long term.

Extendible and retractable issues are sometimes referred to as variable maturity or exchangeable debt. The flexibility inherent in these features has made this type of debt quite popular with investors. This flexibility isn't an attractive feature for issuers, since they do not know in advance whether the securities will be held for the shorter or the longer maturity option.

Factors Affecting Bond Price Movements

So far, we've talked a lot about the price movements of strip bonds. But what about regular bonds? Bond prices and yields in the secondary market are set by the:

- level of interest rates
- credit rating of the issuer
- term to maturity of the issue
- coupon rate of the issue
- features of the issue

Let's look at these one at a time.

The Relationship of Interest Rates to Bond Prices

When interest rates rise, bond prices as a group fall. When interest rates fall, bond prices as a group rise. Such price movements are required to bring bond yields into line with current interest rates, given that the coupon rates do not change. Bond prices are, therefore, subject to the day-to-day fluctuation of the market place.

The Credit Rating of the Issuer

The stronger the financial position of the borrower and the higher its credit rating, the more favorable the terms at which it can borrow. For example, the Government of Canada can borrow at lower cost than a provincial government, and a provincial government can borrow at lower cost than most municipalities. Similarly, a well-known firm can borrow on more favorable terms than a small business.

The stronger the financial position of the borrower and the higher its credit rating, the more favorable the terms on which it can borrow.

Term to Maturity of an Issue

Traditionally, money borrowed for long periods is more costly than money borrowed for short periods. This is logical because more things can happen over a 20-year period to endanger the repayment of the debt than can happen in one year. Investors therefore demand a higher yield to compensate for the higher risk.

A long-term bond also provides another type of risk not present in a short-term bond. This is the exposure to inflation, the great enemy of bonds.

Inflation is the reduction in the purchasing power of money. Ten years ago a dollar would buy you a pound of butter. Now it will buy you a third of a pound. The butter hasn't changed; the value of your dollar has.

It seems inevitable that the value of money will shrink over time;

Canadian Consumer Price Index

Year	Level	Percentage Change	Year	Level	Percentage Change
1986	78.10	4.2	1993	101.80	1.9
1987	81.50	4.3	1994	102.00	0.2
1988	84.80	4.1	1995	104.20	2.2
1989	89.00	5.0	1996	105.90	1.6
1990	93.30	4.8	1997	107.60	1.6
1991	98.50	5.6	1998	108.60	0.9
1992	100.0	1.5	1999	110.45	1.7

the question is, at what rate. The Consumer Price Index, or CPI, is the measure we use to track inflation. It's calculated by adding up the price of a group of household goods. The total price in 1992 was set at 100, and all other years are set relative to that. So the CPI has an absolute number, but it's more commonly compared to what it was last year, so we can see the percentage change.

All those annual increases add up over time. So the longer you have to wait to get your money back, the more chance inflation has to erode its value.

That's why duration is such a key idea. It takes into account the size of coupon payments as well as how long you'll have to wait for them. We should really say, the longer the duration, the greater the inflation risk. Instead, we talk about the longer term. The assumption is that for the most part longer-term bonds have longer durations.

We expect, then, that owing to these risks, a long-term bond will have a higher yield than a short-term bond. Bond analysts use a graph called a yield curve to represent the yields of bonds with differing terms. To compare apples to apples, a yield curve will only use bonds of one issuer, such as the Government of Canada.

As you might expect, long-term bonds will react more strongly to interest rate changes than short-term ones, because the change in their present value would be greater.

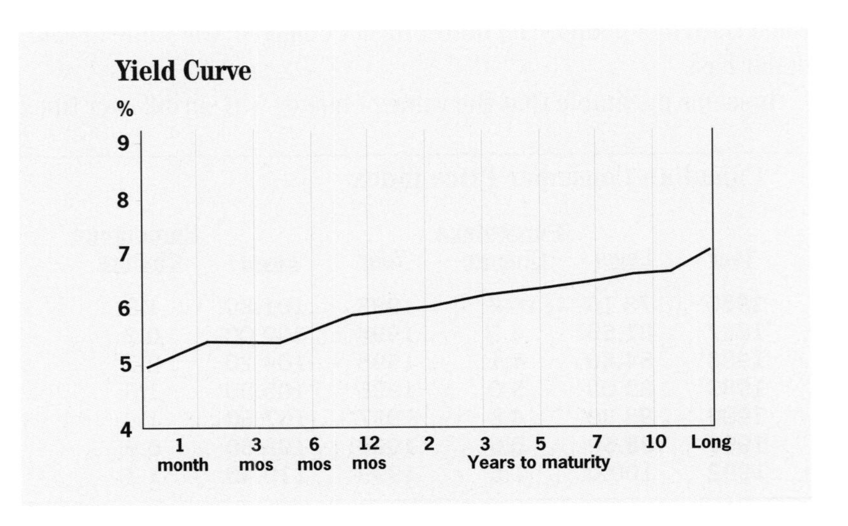

Have a look at our present value chart on page 52. If rates rise from 8% to 10%, the present value of $1 due in six years drops from $0.63 to $0.564, or 10.5%. But at ten years, the drop is from $0.463 to $0.386, or 16.6%. The longer term accentuates the price adjustment.

We can see the same effect illustrated in this chart.

The most volatile bond combines long term and low coupon. The least volatile has a short term and high coupon.

Market Price Volatility

Bond	10% coupon 5 year	Zero coupon 5 year	10% coupon 20 year	Zero coupon 20 year
Price	100	61.39	100	14.20
Yield	10	10	10	10
Price with rate at 7%	112.47	70.89	132.03	25.26
% change	+12.47	+15.47	+32.03	+77.89
Price with rate at 13%	89.22	53.27	78.78	8.05
% change	-10.78	-13.23	-21.22	-43.30

The Coupon Rate of an Issue

As we have seen, a bond with a high coupon will trade at a higher price and with less volatility than a similar bond with a low coupon. The greater the portion of the overall yield that you get over the life of the bond, through the semi-annual coupon payments, the lower the risk and therefore the higher the price.

Features of the Issue

Certain features of a debt issue, such as convertibility or a call provision, can affect its market price. For example, if a debt issue has a sinking fund or purchase fund feature, the fund's market activities may influence the issue's market price. When the fund bids for the issue to retire whatever is bought for sinking or purchase fund purposes, the issue's market price could be favorably affected.

The Yield Curve and Bond Switching

Not only do bond prices and yields fluctuate but also the relationship between short-term and long-term bond yields tends to fluctuate. This latter relationship is easily seen in a yield curve, which continually changes. Because of changing prices and yields as well as changing yield curves, there are often many bond switching opportunities in bond portfolios.

Here is a summary of possible benefits from switches of bonds.

Net yield improvement

There may be opportunities to improve yield after tax without adversely affecting quality. For example, a high tax bracket investor will be better off in deep discount bonds than in high coupon bonds even if the gross yield is the same, because the tax rate on the discount portion of the yield will be based on the capital gains rate and hence lower.

Term extension or reduction

There will be many opportunities in this area due to changing yield curves and to changing requirements.

Improvement in credit

This involves a switch to bonds with a better quality credit. This is particularly possible in corporate bonds, where the prospects for entire industries or particular companies can change radically and sometimes quickly.

Portfolio diversification

Price changes in a portfolio, or the impact of new cash income or cash needs can require reviewing the portfolio. It may need to be further diversified to ensure that risks are spread and not concentrated.

Cash take-outs

These are possible when the proceeds from the sale of a bond exceed the cost of the bond bought with the proceeds. Sometimes it's possible to do this without adversely affecting yield or quality.

Bond Switching Hints

The differing behaviour of bonds with varying coupons and terms enables the astute bond investor to take advantage of interest rate swings by either shortening or lengthening the average term of the bond portfolio. This approach is done by holding a portion of the bond portfolio in long-term low coupon bonds when yields are in the down-ward phase of the interest rate cycle and bond prices are rising. The investor then reverses the position when yields rise and bond prices fall.

The differing behaviour of bonds enables the astute bond investor to take advantage of interest rate swings.

By doing this successfully, a bond investor will make an additional pre-tax return over the average coupon income. However, success will depend on ability to forecast the bond market correctly.

Technical factors related to supply and demand, yield and price spreads for various types of bonds will often make bond switches attractive.

Sinking fund or purchase fund operations often cause temporary distortions in the market that make certain bond switches advantageous.

A sharp rise in the underlying common stock of a convertible debt issue or a debt issue with warrants attached could result in the debt issue selling at a substantial premium above par. In such an instance, a switch to another debt issue could prove advantageous.

The market price of a convertible debt issue might decline once a previously indicated date for a change in conversion terms had passed. In such an instance an opportunity for a bond switch might present itself.

Switches for these and other reasons are a fascinating and continuing aspect of portfolio management.

The Secondary Market

The secondary market buys previously issued bonds.

Now that you are familiar with the main properties of bonds, the next question is where to buy them. And that takes us to the secondary market. In addition to bringing new securities issues to market, investment dealers perform a second major function by trading in the secondary market and by maintaining an inventory of securities. The principal function of this secondary market is to provide a forum for investors to buy previously issued bonds and to sell those they own instead of having to wait for them to mature. An active market allows investors to react to changing economic conditions, not to mention personal circumstances. It also improves primary distribution, since investors can buy new issues and feel confident that they will be able to sell them if need be.

Historically, almost all trading in bonds and debentures in Canada has been conducted on the over-the-counter market, though a few debentures are now traded on the Canadian Venture and Toronto Stock Exchanges. The Canadian bond market is, therefore, an unlisted market and unlisted markets far outstrip the listed stock markets in dollar volume in Canada.

Participants in the Bond Market

Investment dealers trade in the over-the-counter bond market.

Trading in the over-the-counter market is mostly carried on by investment dealers. In a larger investment house the work is divided among several traders. One group handles money market issues, another long-term Government of Canada and provincial bonds, another corporate bonds, and so on.

The sales and trading departments are closely related. Sales people ask for quotations on securities that clients wish to buy or sell, and traders provide them with this information, as well as quotations on securities owned by the firm or available "on the street" – that is to say, at another investment dealer.

Prices on the street market are generally set by negotiation between buying and selling dealers. They will offer to sell securities they own at a slightly higher price than what they paid for them. Another dealer may offer a smaller spread and will presumably make the sale. Where there is a series of bids or offers made in the process of reaching agreement, there is a degree of auction involved. About 100 dealers and a much smaller number of banks and trust companies are active in the street market, which is principally located in Toronto, Montreal and Vancouver. Dealers active in this market are linked to other dealers, banks and large institutional customers by means of the computer systems of five "inter-dealer" bond brokers. Computer screens show the market and size of bid and offering on a wide range of bonds. Dealers can deal through these systems without necessarily knowing the name of the dealer on the other side of the deal until confirmation contracts are exchanged.

The Bank of Canada carries on active open market operations related to its role in the control of the money supply. As a result, the Bank is a major factor in the over-the-counter market for bonds. Traders in Toronto, Montreal, Vancouver and other key centres keep in close touch with Bank of Canada representatives in these cities. The Bank responds only to firm bids and offerings. Dealers are continually in touch with the Bank to test the market by offering or bidding for blocks of Canada bonds.

Market Information

Market information on price, volume, bids and offers is obtained through the inter-dealer computer systems already mentioned or by traders talking to each other. Printed information is also provided by some dealers who issue daily, weekly or monthly quotation sheets, and by the bond quotations supplied by various investment dealers to daily and weekly financial newspapers and wire services.

The Securities Firm as Dealer

An effective secondary market is dependent on many dealers who wish to make markets and trade in securities and are prepared to take positions in securities. Trading creates liquidity which is essential for a good secondary market. High volumes attract more participation in the market since buyers and sellers can trade, whenever they wish, at competitive prices. If you know that the underwriter will bid for a security you have bought, you'll have more confidence in the security and in the underwriter. By the same token, other dealers will get in touch with the dealer calling a firm market to buy or sell that particular security.

If you decide to sell a bond at a certain price, your investment advisor will notify the bond trader of your offering. The trader will subtract a fraction of a point from this offering price as profit and make a firm bid for the bond. Should you wish to buy bonds, the trader will add a fraction to the price and make a firm offering.

Securities acquired and held by dealers in the course of trading, or as the odds and ends of new issues, become part of the firms' inventory, otherwise known as a long position. Inventory is sometimes acquired as a result of a new issue moving slowly, or as a service to clients who wish to dispose of securities.

The size of the inventory carried is usually set by the dealer's assessment of the general market at the time and by its need to maintain reserves for possible future commitments. It's also related to the dealer's own capital because of the Investment Dealers Association's minimum capital regulations which require the margining of inventory held.

The Securities Firm as Trading Agent

Underwriting dealers act as trading agents and help an issuing company fulfill its sinking fund or purchase fund obligations.

Another function of an underwriting dealer is to act as trading agent and help an issuing company fulfill its sinking fund or purchase fund obligations (these are funds specifically set aside to repay or retire an issuer's debt securities). This gives such a dealer an advantage in calling markets in securities it has underwritten for the issuing company. The dealer is enabled to maintain an orderly market in these securities which in turn will facilitate further new issues.

Purpose of a Bond Trading Department

In summary then, the purpose and function of a bond trading department is:

- to help in the original offerings of securities to the public by absorbing securities taken in exchange for new issues, and by maintaining marketability for new issues to the greatest extent possible during and following original offerings;

- to make or get competitive bids on securities and to offer or get securities on a competitive basis for the investor or speculator, thereby making it possible for the seller or buyer to complete transactions with a minimum of delay;
- to manage the investment dealer's own security position or inventory;
- to gain, particularly by contact with other bond dealers, relevant information related to the bond market, which will help in trading or in allowing new underwritings to be properly priced.

Regulation of Bond Trading

As an over-the-counter market, there's no physical location in Canada in which bonds are bought and sold. Even so, the bond market is carefully regulated through the Investment Dealers Association. Their rules cover all major aspects of trading such as: trading practices, including full details of sizes to be traded; trading units and rules on delivery practices, including rules on regular delivery; accrued interest and good delivery; buy-ins, and general regulations concerned with the trading and delivery of bonds, debentures and unlisted stocks.

There's no physical location in Canada in which bonds are bought and sold.

Settlement

In the old days, buyers would normally get a bond certificate after paying for it - known as settlement - and hold it in safekeeping while they owned the bond. Nowadays the settlement for most bonds is handled for most banks, trust companies and investment dealers by the same agency that handles stock settlements, The Canadian Depository for Securities Limited, or CDS. If you buy a bond for which a certificate is still available, the settlement procedure is done through a Certificate Based System. If you don't want to get a certificate, a computerized settlement procedure called a Book Based System is used. Under this system, the certificate is held in the CDS vault and a computerized entry keeps track of your name. The entry will appear on the computer of the bank, trust company or investment dealer with whom you deal as well as in CDS records. Many bonds owned by institutions are held on a book-based system and many retail buyers also choose be on this system.

Taxation of Bond Income

When you buy or sell bonds, accrued interest is included in the total amount. Interest accrues from the last interest payment date up to the settlement date. As the seller, you would get this amount from the buyer. The buyer would regain this interest at the next interest payment date or if they sell the bond in the meantime.

Bonds which are bought or sold without accrued interest are said to have been traded flat.

Accrued Interest

On June 16 you buy $20,000 of 8.00% ACME Ltd. bonds due Sept. 1 2004. Interest accrues from March 2 (the day after the most recent semi-annual interest date) to June 19 (settlement date – three business days after the trade date). Number of days of accrued interest:

March 2-31	30 days
April	30 days
May	31 days
June	19 days
TOTAL	110 days

Accrued interest calculation:

$$\frac{\$20{,}000}{1} \times \frac{8.00}{100} \times \frac{110}{365} = \$482.19$$

As you might expect, there are tax implications on accrued interest. If you are the seller of a bond, you'll be taxed on any accrued interest that is included in the payment you get from the buyer. For the buyer, the total accrued interest paid on buying bonds or debentures is a recognized deduction from total interest received. You should keep contract notes covering purchases and sales of bonds so that you can file accurate income tax returns.

In some cases, a taxpayer might get interest payment for a

period that spans more than one tax year. For example, let's say you get a six-month interest payment for a period that starts on August 1 of one year and ends on February 28 of the next.

Fortunately, Revenue Canada keeps things fairly simple. You are considered to get interest from a fully registered bond as of the date of the interest cheque, so you don't have to figure out how much of the money was earned in the previous year and how much in the current year.

Taxation of Capital Gains

Canadian tax laws generally provide that interest income from debt securities is taxed as income at your personal tax rate. Interest income has no equivalent to the federal Dividend Tax Credit which gives you a break on dividends from stocks.

Sale or redemption of a bond can result in a taxable capital gain or allowable capital loss. Your gain or loss is the difference between the proceeds you get on the sale and the adjusted cost base. If you were selling a treasury bill though, the price gain is regarded as interest income, which is taxed at your personal tax rate.

Adjusted Cost Base

What, you may ask, is the adjusted cost base? Quite simply, it's either the amount that you paid for a bond, or it's the weighted average price of a bond bought at different prices on different dates.

Bonds trading significantly below par are particularly desirable for most high tax-bracket individuals since a substantial portion of

Adjusted Cost Base

Purchase Date	Face Value	Price	Cost
June 1	$10,000	96	9,600
July 2	$5,000	98	4,900
Total	$15,000		14,500
Adjusted Cost Base		96.67	

their return is regarded as capital gain, of which only 67% is taxable. The advantage is greater for high tax-bracket individuals than for others, since their tax rate is higher. The capital gains rate isn't normally applicable to "traders" who are in and out of the market all the time. Their gains are regarded as a regular part of their income and taxed as such.

The Attraction of Zero Coupon or Strip Bonds

Most bonds pay interest twice a year. But there is one type of bond that does not. In fact, it pays no interest at all. Not only that – you have to pay tax on the interest that you didn't get.

You might wonder why anyone in their right mind would buy such a bond. But strip bonds, or zero-coupon bonds as they are sometimes called, have another unique feature. And that is the ability to lock in a compounded reinvestment rate and thereby avoid one of the biggest dangers of bonds – reinvestment risk.

To understand strip bonds, it helps to think of a regular bond as a series of payments promised to the holder. Let's go back to our $5,000 8% six-year bond. It consists of 12 twice-yearly $200 payments for the next six years, and a $5,000 payment at the end of that time. When we buy the bond, we're buying all those promises to pay.

Now imagine that those 13 payments were sold individually. For instance, what if you could buy one of those $200 coupons by itself? You would be buying what we call a zero coupon bond.

Zeros first appeared in Canada in 1982. They are usually created by a dealer acquiring a block of existing high quality federal or provincial government bonds and then physically separating the individual coupons from the bond certificate. Each coupon is then sold separately at significant discounts to its face value. The certificate itself, which is now called the residue, representing the principal amount, is also sold separately. In effect it too becomes a zero coupon bond.

Holders of strip bonds get no interest payments. Instead, you buy the bonds at a discount at a price that will result in a certain

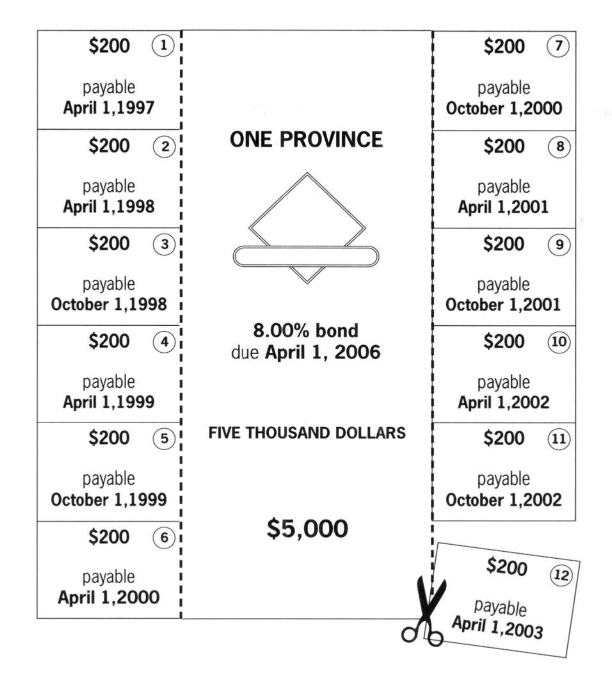

compounded rate of return. Given a specified interest rate and term to maturity, you can use a Present Value Factor table to get an appropriate price. For example, if you wanted to get a compounded rate of return of 8% on a coupon due in six years with a face value of $200, you would pay $0.63 per $1 face value, or (0.63 X 200) $126. In return for giving up the regular cash flow that semi-annual interest payments provide, you lock in a compounded rate of return.

The Magic of Compound Interest

Compound interest is interest paid on interest.

Compound interest is interest paid on interest. The interest that the zero coupon bond doesn't pay you is added to the principal. This larger amount then earns interest, which in turn accumulates and earns interest. The present value table uses compound interest calculations. For example, if you take the $0.63 from the table and add 8%, you get $0.68 which is the 8%, five-year number. And adding 8% to that will give you $0.735, the next number up the chart. If you keep adding 8% you'll get back to the $1 at the top of the chart. That's compounding. It can make your money grow at a rapid rate; some people refer to "the magic of compounding". Compound interest can have a significant effect on an investment. For example, have another look at the table, this time at the 12% column. The present value of a one-dollar payment due in six years is .507. Thus, at 12%, you could invest 50.7 cents and it would be worth a dollar in six years. Your money would have doubled in that time period.

Keep in mind that a 12% return on your money is hard to do right now, although in the early 1980s it would have been easy. As well, there are some other characteristics of strips that you should consider before purchasing them. The securities administrators agree, because they require that first-time purchasers be given a special Purchase Circular, or Information Statement. The Circular must address some of the ways in which zeros differ from other bonds. Among these are income tax consequences, the extent of the secondary market and price volatility.

Present Value Factor tables – single payments

The present value of an isolated $1 payment due in X years time is calculated using the following present value (or discount) rates (rounded to 3 decimals):

Year	5%	8%	10%	12%	Year	5%	8%	10%	12%
1	.952	.926	.909	.893	11	.585	.429	.350	.287
2	.907	.857	.826	.797	12	.557	.397	.319	.257
3	.864	.794	.751	.712	13	.530	.368	.290	.229
4	.823	.735	.683	.636	14	.505	.341	.263	.205
5	.784	.681	.621	.567	15	.481	.315	.239	.183
6	.746	.630	.564	.507	16	.458	.292	.218	.163
7	.711	.583	.513	.452	17	.436	.270	.198	.146
8	.677	.540	.467	.404	18	.416	.250	.180	.130
9	.645	.500	.424	.361	19	.396	.232	.164	.116
10	.614	.463	.386	.322	20	.377	.215	.149	.104

Taxation of Zeros

As we mentioned earlier, you must declare income from these bonds every year even though you get no interest payments. This is called deemed interest. But how do you work out how much interest to report if you didn't actually get any?

Our present value table can help us here. Let's say you buy the $5,000 bond residue from our example. It matures in six years. You might pay $3,150 for it. If you divide 3,150 by 5,000 you'll see that our discount factor is .63, which appears in the six-year row in the 8% column.

A year later, with five years until maturity, the discount rate is .681, and the value of the residue should be .681 times 5,000, or $3,405. The theoretical value of the residue has increased from $3,150 to $3,405, or $255. You would report $255 of interest income on your tax return.

The Secondary Market

The securities administrators want investors to realize that zeros trade on the over-the-counter market like other bonds. As such there's no guarantee that there will be a healthy market for any particular coupon. However, the market has grown dramatically in the 1990s, so it's unlikely that investors will not be able to trade their coupons.

Price Volatility

The administrators also want you to know that a zero coupon bond will be more volatile than a conventional bond with the same term and risk. Let's see why this is the case.

Say you buy a conventional $5,000, 8% bond due in six years. If you hold the bond to maturity you can expect to get your $5,000 principal plus interest of $400 dollars a year or $2,400 over six years. That's a total of $7,400.

Thus, a conventional bond gives your money back in installments. In this example, the interest payments represent 32.4% of the total, and you would get them semi-annually over the five years.

Zero coupon bonds are riskier and more volatile than a conventional bond.

In contrast, a zero makes you wait for five years before you see any of your money and that's why it's more volatile. For instance, if you paid $3,150 for the $5,000 residue of our sample bond you would not see any money until the six-year mark. In the meantime, the entire value of the zero will fluctuate relative to changes in interest rates. Thus, zeros are riskier and more volatile than a conventional bond.

The Concept of Duration

There is a technical name for what we are talking about – bond analysts would call it duration. Duration is the average term of all the bond payments – coupons and principal – weighted by the amount of the payment and its present value. Duration for a zero is simple: since there's only one payment, its duration is the same as its term. The duration of our 8%, six-year bond is a little more complicated to figure out but we know it will be less than six years, because you are getting some of your money back along the way. To be exact, you'll be getting 29.7% of it during the term of the bond (not 32.4%, because the payment date for the final $200 coupon is at maturity, along with the $5,000 principal).

In simple terms, duration is the average amount of time you have to wait to get your money back. In the case of our 8%, six-year bond, the duration is 4.88 years.

In simple terms, duration is the average amount of time you have to wait to get your money back.

Now, you might be wondering: if you start getting your money back with the first coupon payment six months from now, get several evenly spaced payments after that, and get the last payment along with principal when the bond matures in six years, why would the duration not be 3.25 years, which is the average time of the 12 payments?

That would be true if duration calculations did not also consider the amount and present value of each payment. Your last payment is by far the largest, since it includes the principal, so even though its present value factor is the smallest, it still ends up weighting the scale past the natural mid-point.

Why Zeros are More Volatile

Let's return for a moment to volatility to better illustrate a mathematical reason why zeros have wider price fluctuations. Let's look at our 8% six-year bond again. Assume a year has gone by, and interest rates are still at 8%. Our bond would have to be at 100 to yield 8%. Bonds will always move in price to reflect current interest rates. Since the coupon is fixed, it's the price that must change to keep the yield in line with changes in rates.

For example, let's say rates have risen to 9%. You probably

wouldn't be interested in buying our 8% bond, not when you could buy a newly issued one and get 9%.

However, if our bond changed its price so that it also yielded 9%; then you might feel differently. If it was priced at less than 100, its yield would increase.

Of course, to get 9%, you would have to get some of your return in the form of a capital gain. Keep that in mind for later when we talk about how the coupon affects volatility: the more of the yield that is obtained through the coupon, the less of it that has to be realized through a price change. And as we've discussed, the greater interest payment portion of the yield, the lower the volatility.

Ignoring volatility for the moment, the question becomes: how big a capital gain will you need for your 8% six-year bond to yield 9%.

Fortunately, there are formulas that will tell you the price you would pay for an 8%, six-year bond so that your yield would be 9%,

Pricing a $5,000 8% six-year bond when interest rates are at 9%.

Payments Face Value	Term	Discount Rate (rounded)	Present Value
200	0.5	0.958	191.57
200	1.0	0.917	183.49
200	1.5	0.879	175.75
200	2.0	0.842	168.34
200	2.5	0.806	161.24
200	3.0	0.772	154.44
200	3.5	0.740	147.92
200	4.0	0.708	141.69
200	4.5	0.679	135.71
200	5.0	0.650	129.99
200	5.5	0.623	124.50
200	6.0	0.596	119.25
5,000	6.0	0.596	2,981.34
Total			4,815.21

$4,815.21 is 96.30% of the $5,000 face value: the bond would be priced at 96.30.

or, for that matter, the price you would pay for any bond to give you a particular yield. These formulas work out the net present value of each coupon and the principal, using whatever interest rate you specify. They then add up all these values, which gives you the total present worth of the bond. Dividing by the face value gives you a price relative to 100.

As you can see by our chart, the net present value of all the bond's payments is $4,815.21. That's 96.3% of face value, so to get a 9% yield from that bond, you would have to buy it at 96.30.

In a way, it looks as if we have taken our 8% bond and turned it into 13 zero coupon bonds. This should not be surprising because when you buy a bond you are buying a series of future payments, each one of which resembles a zero coupon bond. And bonds are priced in the same way as zeros, except they have more than one part to deal with.

According to the chart, if you pay 96.30 for this bond, or $4,815 for the $5,000 face value, you'll be getting a 9% yield. Let's double-check this figure with a rough yield calculation.

The numerator is the $8 coupon plus the annual gain on the price change from 96.30 to 100. That gain is $3.70, which is $0.617 annually. So our numerator is $8.617.

The denominator is the average of 100 and 96.30. That's 98.15.

So our calculation would look like this:

$$\frac{8.617}{98.15} = 8.78\%$$

Now you can see why they call it a rough yield calculation, although it's not too bad when you consider the amount of work that went into preparing the present value chart.

Now let's look at the effect an interest rate change would have on a zero coupon bond.

In our earlier example, we talked about buying the $5,000 residue at 63, which would give us an 8% yield over six years. What if interest rates went to 9%?

The discount rate for a six-year term at 9% is .596; so the residue would drop to 59.60 from 63.

So on a percentage basis, our zero would suffer more than the regular bond from a 1% rise in rates. The zero went down 5.40%, whereas in dropping from 100 to 96.30, the regular bond lost 3.70%.

How Zeros Eliminate Reinvestment Risk

A few pages back, we mentioned that one of benefits of zeros was that they allow you to avoid re-investment risk. By re-investment risk, we mean the danger that you'll be unable to re-invest your interest payments at rates equivalent to or higher than those paid on your original investment.

Now don't misunderstand us. We all like the thought of getting money regularly. But think of a portfolio manager with millions of dollars in bonds. The coupon payments would be substantial. In fact, on a long-term bond, the total coupon payments far exceed the principal. And whatever the coupon rate, the manager will only be able to reinvest the payments at the going rate at the time they are received. Yet that reinvestment rate is a huge factor in the bond's total return.

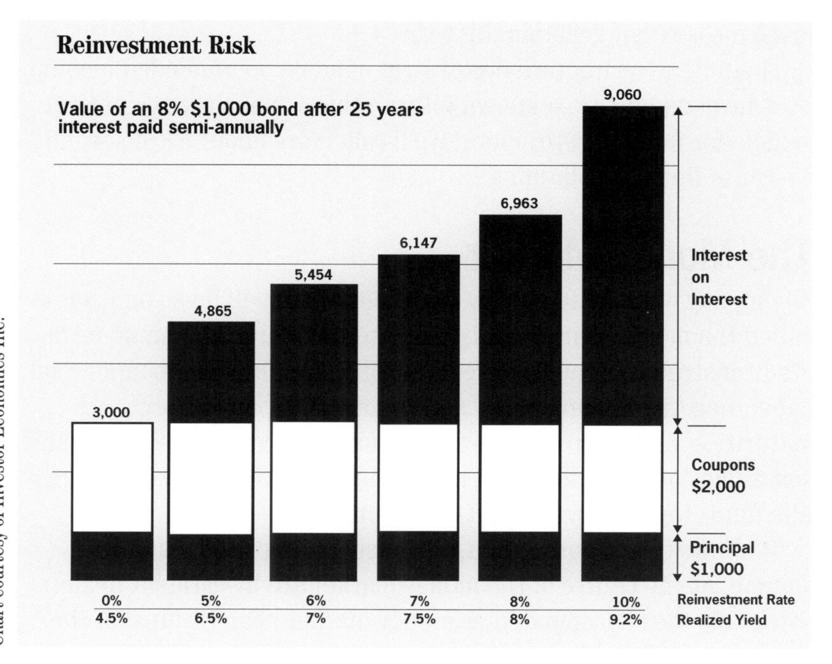

Chart courtesy of Investor Economics Inc.

In contrast, zero coupon bonds do not have interest payments, so there's nothing to reinvest. When you buy the bond, you have already locked in the rate at which the money will compound. You know how much you'll end up with. A regular bond doesn't give you that luxury because you never know the rate at which you can reinvest the coupon proceeds.

For someone who needs to know exactly what their investment will be worth a few years down the road, strip bonds seem like a great thing. But the idea of paying taxes on money you didn't even get means they aren't for everyone, especially if they are held in a taxable account.

Why Zeros are Ideal for RRSPs

When it comes to self-directed RRSPs, however, strip bonds can be an attractive investment. Investment returns aren't taxed inside an RRSP, so that eliminates the zero coupon tax problem. And as well, your RRSP investments shouldn't be geared to current income, since you are probably not going to touch the money at least until you retire. You should be more concerned with their value in the future than how much income they generate this year.

The unique characteristics of strip bonds – no unneeded income, no reinvestment risk, a known future value – make them a perfect vehicle for funding retirement. We'll talk more about RRSPs when we get to financial planning.

The Money Market

A company wanting to borrow for a short term will do so on what is called the money market. This refers to the market for short-term credit instruments such as treasury bills, non-financial commercial paper, negotiable bank paper and finance company paper. Maturities may be up to one year but usually are 90 days or less and sometimes only one day. This market brings those with temporarily idle funds together with short-term borrowers.

The money market allows quick, convenient, low-cost trading in almost any volume.

It allows quick, convenient, low-cost trading in almost any volume. At the centre of the money market are investment dealers, especially those designated as money market dealers. Most of the activity occurs in Toronto and Montreal and is conducted by telephone, making the market easily accessible to all parts of the country as well as to foreign financial centres.

Participants in the Money Market

Participants in the money market are those who enter the market to raise short-term funds or to invest cash surpluses. Funds may be raised by selling holdings of money market instruments, by borrowing from financial institutions (usually chartered banks) or by issuing new short-term debt instruments. Such borrowers must have high and accepted credit standings. Suppliers of funds in the money market are those who buy money market instruments or make short-term loans, that is, those whose cash needs are some time in the future and can earn some interest income by holding interest-bearing liquid assets instead of non-earning cash. Participants include all levels of government, chartered banks and other financial institutions, finance companies, non-financial corporations and individuals.

The money market provides both users and suppliers of capital a choice of how they borrow or invest. Users may borrow from their bankers or they may issue money market securities. Suppliers, on the other hand, may deposit their cash with their banker or acquire securities. Greater flexibility enables participants to proceed in the way that's more advantageous to them. Market interest rates often enable borrowers using the money market to borrow for less than from the banks. You can often earn higher rates of return from money market instruments than by depositing funds in bank accounts. The choices available to users and suppliers of capital has created a highly competitive and efficient money market.

The money market provides both users and suppliers of capital choice of how they borrow or invest.

How Money Market Instruments Work

Most money market instruments have some common characteristics. Denominations are usually in $100,000 multiples, but some notes are available in amounts as low as $1,000. Most paper has a stated maturity, but the term of corporate paper can be negotiated and some issues may be cashed in advance of maturity, although usually for a lower rate of return. Because of their short-term nature, these securities do not usually pay interest as such. Instead, you buy them for less then their maturity value – at a discount – and hold them until they mature at par.

For example, let's say you have $10,000 to invest. You might see a money market security with a maturity of three months trading at 98. The maturity value is 100, so you could spend $9,800 and buy $10,000 of that security. Now you just have to wait three months until it matures at 100, or $10,000. You have made $200 on your $9,800 investment, and you have done it in 90 days, or one quarter of a year. Your return or yield is 2.04% in 90 days or, on an annualized basis, about 8.16%.

Types of Money Market Instruments

A wide variety of money market instruments is issued by both the government and the private sector. A brief description of the most common types is provided below.

Treasury bills are virtually risk-free and thus acceptable to all lenders.

Government of Canada Treasury Bills

Treasury bills are the focal point of the money market because they are virtually risk-free and thus acceptable to all lenders. They are liquid, and large volumes can be bought and sold quickly without significant yield change. New bills are auctioned every week. Accordingly, it's quite simple to acquire outstanding bills or to bid for new issues with approximately the desired term. T-bills, as they are known, are normally issued with terms of 91, 182 and 364 days.

Government of Canada Bonds (due in three years or less)

If the government issued a bond eight years ago that would mature in ten years, it would now only have two years left until maturity. Thus, this type of bond would also trade on the money market, even though it wasn't created as a money market instrument.

The quality of these bonds is the same as that of treasury bills, but liquidity generally tends to be somewhat lower.

Provincial and Municipal Short-term Paper

Provinces issue paper on their own authority and can also authorize their wholly-owned Crown corporations to issue short-term instruments. Municipal governments also borrow under their own authority. Credit ratings vary and liquidity is usually somewhat limited. At one time or another all the provinces have issued treasury bills, as have many of their Crown corporations, but only the largest municipalities have entered this market.

Finance Company (or Acceptance) Paper

Finance companies were the first to issue paper and become regular short-term borrowers in the market. In some cases, the paper is secured by specific assets such as installment obligations of the companies' customers; in other cases, the backing is the general credit of the issuer. Paper is usually issued through investment dealers. Terms are often negotiable.

Commercial Paper (Non-financial Corporations)

This is how your average corporation borrows money on a short-term basis. Commercial paper isn't specifically secured but is usually supported by stand-by lines of credit at the issuers' bankers. In some cases (which also apply to finance companies) there is a parent company guarantee. As in the case of finance company paper, commercial paper is issued in interest bearing or discount form with terms of a few days to a year. It's usually placed through investment dealers who may act as principals or as agents. Some paper may also be placed directly with lenders by the non-financial borrower.

Bankers' Acceptances

A bankers' acceptance is a commercial draft, or a written instruction to make payment, issued by a non-financial corporation that has been accepted by the borrower's bank. Accepted here means that the payment of interest and principal is guaranteed by the borrower's bank. Bankers consider acceptances carrying their mark to be liabilities of the bank, but the issuer must make funds available to the bank on the maturity date. The market yield on acceptances is usually a little lower than on commercial paper because they are backed by the credit of the issuer as well as by its bank, but the accepting fee charged by the banks makes the cost of borrowing the money a little higher. Paper is usually issued on a discount basis through money market dealers who may act as agents or principals.

Chartered Bank Paper

Canadian chartered banks issue a wide variety of deposit instruments designed to attract deposits from those with cash to invest. Most of them are modifications of passbook deposits. Bearer deposit notes or bearer term notes are types of bank paper traded in the money market. They are transferable and are sold and traded on a discount basis. In most cases, these notes are issued by banks directly to their customers.

Non-transferable Vehicles

In addition to the marketable instruments just described, there are non-transferable vehicles for investment which usually are registered in the investor's name and carry a specific rate of return for a specific term. Some are redeemable prior to maturity with an interest rate reduction. The largest of these are trust company Guaranteed Investment Certificates – GICs, and chartered bank Certificates of Deposit – CDs.

Swapped Deposits

The chartered banks also offer swapped deposits. Such a transaction consists of a spot purchase of foreign currency, usually U.S. dollars, with the proceeds deposited at the bank for a specified period and bearing an appropriate rate of interest. At the time of the spot purchase, a forward sale is made in the same account for a future date identical to the maturity date of the deposit and, thus, the investor has a fully hedged foreign currency deposit. The rate of return is the rate on the deposit, plus or minus the spread on the exchange swap.

You can see that the money market operates in a highly flexible way to maximize the use of available but temporarily idle funds. It serves a broad spectrum of borrowers and lenders, and new instruments and techniques are constantly being developed. It has grown greatly in size and sophistication in a comparatively short period.

While most investors can see the potential to make money by buying and selling bonds, such opportunities are harder to recognize in money market. There, the term of most securities is short and price fluctuations are minor. While it's true that short-term bonds won't fluctuate in price as much as long term bonds, it doesn't take much of a price change to realize a decent profit when you are trading millions of dollars in market instruments.

When people think about securities markets, they tend to concentrate on the stock market alone. In this chapter, we've tried to show you that the bond market is also worthy of your attention. And that learning about the forces that drive it can increase your understanding of the equity markets.

Summary

Borrowed money is one of the two major parts of a firm's capital structure. Much of this money is acquired through the issuance of bonds and debentures. These debt issues have certain characteristics such as semi-annual interest payments, a maturity date, a redemption feature, and denomination size. Once issued, bonds trade on an over-the-counter secondary market. This market is regulated by the IDA and investment dealers are key participants in it.

Bond interest is taxed at the holder's regular tax rate. Sixty-seven percent of any capital gains that arise from selling a bond are taxable at the seller's regular rate.

A bond is a series of promises to pay specified amounts of money at specified times. How much are all of those promises worth today? To find out, we must find out the present value of each payment, be it a coupon or the principal, given today's interest rates. The bond will be worth the sum of the present value of all these payments. We can then compare this value to the bond's market price to see if a buying opportunity exists. Zero coupon bonds are also priced exactly this way, except there is only one payment to deal with. Zeros have some characteristics that make them different than regular bonds. They don't pay interest, there are differing tax considerations, they are more volatile than regular bonds, and their compounding aspect eliminates reinvestment risk.

Bond prices fluctuate along with interest rates. Since a bond's coupon payment is fixed, it's the price that must change to bring the bond's yield into line with current rates. Other factors that affect bond prices are the issuer's credit rating, the term, the coupon rate and whether the bond has any special features. Investors can use bond switching to take advantage of price fluctuations.

There are several ways to classify bonds. One way is by the security behind the issue: from a first mortgage bond to a subordinated debenture. Another is by the bond's features: extendible, retractable, sinking or purchase fund, or convertible. A conversion feature probably has the largest affect on a bond's value, as it links the bond to the price movements of the firm's common shares. Conversion cost premium and payback period formula can help to evaluate a convertible's worth.

The money market is the part of the bond market where short-term debt is traded. Treasury bills are the most important money market instrument, but there is a variety of other government and corporate issues that trade there.

Stocks

Features of common and preferred shares and how to choose them.

In the previous chapter, we talked about investing in a company by loaning it money, through such instruments as bonds and debentures. There is, however, a more fundamental way of investing in a firm, and that's by buying its stock therefore becoming one of the owners of the company.

Investing in a company's "equity capital" can be a rewarding way to participate in a firm's success, but it can also be much riskier. If the company performs well, the value of its stock could skyrocket – every investor's dream – and you could reap a small fortune. But if it fails, the value of the stock could tumble to pennies, or to nothing.

Always remember that a firm must pay off its debts – including bank loans and interest owed on bonds and debentures – before its owners see a cent in dividends. And if it fails and has to be liquidated, the creditors have first claim on the assets. As a shareholder, you are entitled to whatever is left. And that could be nothing at all.

With this caution ringing in your ears, let's talk about the advantages of buying stock. The first part of our discussion will focus on common shares; later we'll talk about preferred shares, rights and warrants.

Ownership of the common stock of a firm is usually accompanied by the right to a say in the way the company is run.

Common Shares

Ownership of the common stock of a firm is usually – but not always – accompanied by the right to a say in the way the company is run. This includes the right to attend the annual meeting, to elect the directors who guide and control the business operations, and to vote on special questions, such as the sale, merger or liquidation of the business or the amendment of the charter.

Voting Rights

Usually, each common shareholder has one vote for each share owned.

To vote, you must have shares issued in your own name or be in possession of a completed proxy form. Usually, each common shareholder has one vote for each share owned. Shareholders often sign proxy forms giving company management their vote. Even so, an annual meeting is a valuable opportunity to question management and make your views known. And there's always the possibility of the high drama of a "proxy fight", with management and challengers campaigning for proxy support before or during a meeting.

Potential for Capital Appreciation

When a company "goes public", its stock becomes available to the public, normally through a listing on a stock exchange, or by trading in an OTC market. Investors are free to buy and sell the firm's shares; depending on its performance and prospects, the market value of the stock can rise or fall, possibly many times. If you "buy low, sell high" – always the preferred scenario – you profit from your investment with a capital gain when you sell.

A stock's price can rise substantially over time in response to several factors including a firm's earnings record and its prospects for growth in the future. Most companies believe it's good corporate strategy to keep the market price of their shares in a popular price range, say $20-$50. Past that point, companies will consider a stock split or subdivision to bring the price back into the preferred range.

Stock Splits

The mechanics of a stock split are straightforward. First, the company's directors pass and submit a by-law for approval by a vote of the voting common shareholders at a special meeting. Depending on the current market price of the shares, the split could be on any basis such as two new shares for one old share; or three new for one old; or even ten for one. When a split becomes effective, the market price of the new shares reflects the basis of the split.

After a split is first announced, the initial effect on the market price of the stock may be bullish. There can be a modest surge in the price of the shares on increased volume. Dividend increases, often announced at the same time, contribute to the initial bullish impact. The effect of a split on the share's market price after the initial flurry depends on several key factors, such as the firm's earnings trend and the current stage of the stock market cycle.

Reverse Stock Splits

Alternately, a company may do a reverse stock split or consolidation, reducing each shareholder's total shareholdings in the firm. Reverse splits occur most often among low-priced junior mining and oil exploration companies.

A reverse split raises the market price of the new shares and can put the firm in a better position to raise new exploration capital.

Marketability

To make (or lose) money when selling stock, you have to find someone willing to buy it from you. That's usually not a hard thing to accomplish; you can find a buyer for most Canadian securities (in reasonable quantities) within a day or so – if you can agree on a price. It's a simple matter with few legal formalities.

The Stock Exchanges

Bringing buyers and sellers together in a way that will ensure a fair and efficient trade is the responsibility of the world's traditional stock exchanges.

The world's traditional stock exchanges brings buyers and sellers together.

There are about 200 traditional exchanges in over 60 nations around the world, including the three in Canada: the Montreal Exchange, the Toronto Stock Exchange and the Canadian Venture Exchange with offices in Vancouver and Calgary. Most of these exchanges are operated as auction markets in which all trades are exposed to the exchange's entire order book. In this way, each investor can be assured that their order was filled at the best available price.

In the past few years, dramatic advances in desktop computing and data transmission have also spurred the development of Alternative Trading Systems (ATSs). An ATS is a privately owned computer system that routes and matches orders electronically, outside the auspices of the traditional exchanges.

Today, ATSs account for a rapidly growing share of securities trading in the U.S. and the regulatory framework that will allow their operation in Canada is imminent. Because ATSs use recent technology and do not incur many of the regulatory expenses borne by traditional exchanges, they are able to offer individual investors a low-cost alternative for buying and selling shares. ATSs are also attractive to institutional investors because they allow anonymous trading. That makes it easier for pension funds and other money managers to trade large volumes of shares without adversely affecting their price.

How the Stock Exchange Works

During trading hours, Canada's exchanges get thousands of buy and sell orders from all parts of the country and abroad. The process begins when you place an order with your broker to sell or buy shares. If the proposed price is acceptable, the order is usually quickly matched by someone else's buy or sell order, delivered through their broker, and the transaction is completed. Each broker gets a commission from their client for putting through the trade.

The Over-the-Counter Market

The OTC market is a way of buying and selling securities by negotiations as well as by auction.

There is also trading through the Over-the-Counter (OTC) Market, otherwise known as the unlisted market. Although complete statistics aren't available, the volume of unlisted equity business in Canada is smaller than the volume of stock exchange transactions. Many junior issues trade OTC on the Canadian Dealing Network (CDN), but so do the shares of a few conservative industrial companies whose boards of directors have for one reason or another decided not to seek stock exchange listing for one or more issues of their equities.

Over-the-counter trading in equities is conducted in a similar way to bond trading. One veteran described the OTC market as a "market without a marketplace", a way of buying and selling securities by negotiation as well as by auction, which is the method used on stock exchanges. A network of telephones and computer equipment effectively links hundreds of brokers and investment dealers all over the country. Transactions over this network are carried out by traders who specialize in OTC securities. Trading goes on for longer than stock exchange hours, and in a busy market can take up an entire business day.

How Stock Trading Benefits Issuers

When a company first sells its shares to investors, the proceeds from the sale go to the firm. When these outstanding shares are subsequently sold by their holders, the selling price is paid to the seller of the shares and not to the corporation. Shares, therefore, may be transferred from one owner to another without affecting the operations of the company or its finances. That's fine for the investors, but how does such a transaction benefit the firm that issued the shares in the first place?

A strong share price enhances a firm's financial strength and flexibility.

The simple answer is that the stronger the share price, the easier it will be for that company to raise more capital by selling more shares in the future. What's more, a stronger share price enhances a firm's financial strength and flexibility. For example, a company might want to purchase another firm using its own shares as currency for the acquisition. These are just two of the many reasons that companies tend to keep a close eye on their share price.

Companies may also purchase some or all of their own common shares either by tender or on the open market for cancellation, subsequent resale, or for use in dividend reinvestment plans. This practice is popularly known as a buy-back.

Constraints

In some circumstances, there may be constraints on the marketability of shares. Stock exchanges and securities commissions have the power to halt or suspend trading in a company's shares pending a major development, an important announcement or an investigation of a firm's affairs. In some cases, the sale of shares of certain companies to persons who are not Canadian citizens or not residents of Canada is restricted. These companies, known as constrained share companies, include banks, trust and insurance companies, and broadcasting and communications companies.

The Benefits of Investing in Stock

As we mentioned earlier, one of the best reasons to own stock is the capital appreciation that reflects a company's growing fortunes. As an equity investor, however, you'll also enjoy several other benefits.

The Right to Receive Dividends

If a company performs well, you may have the happy experience of seeing it post a profit. If it's a fast-growing business, or in a period of expansion, its directors may decide to plough the profits back into the business. A more mature firm, however, will likely share some or all the good fortune with its owners, through the declaration of dividends.

Unlike interest on debt, dividends on common shares are not a contractual obligation. The board of directors decides whether to pay a dividend, as well as the amount and payment date. An announcement is made in advance of the payment date. Companies may pay dividends quarterly, semi-annually or annually.

Some companies paying common share dividends designate a specified amount that will be paid each year as a regular dividend. The term regular indicates to investors that payments will be maintained barring a major collapse in earnings.

Dividend Reinvestment Plans

Some major companies give their preferred and common shareholders the option of participating in an automatic Dividend Reinvestment Plan. In such a plan, the firm diverts the shareholders' dividends to buy more shares of the company. The result is a kind of automatic savings plan, which solves the problem of reinvesting small amounts of cash. Participating shareholders acquire a gradually increasing share position in the firm, and, because purchases by the plan are made regularly, the advantages of dollar cost averaging are obtained. In addition, purchases made through dividend reinvestment plans are free of commission.

Unfortunately, reinvested dividends are taxable to the shareholder as ordinary cash dividends even though the dividends are not received as cash.

Favorable Tax Treatment of Dividends and Capital Gains

The tax system in Canada provides three incentives for investing in common shares:

- only 67% of capital gains on an investment are subject to income tax, at the investors normal rate
- the federal dividend tax credit, makes buying dividend-paying shares of taxable Canadian companies attractive, particularly for persons in lower tax brackets;
- stock savings plans, which entitle residents of several provinces to deduct up to a set amount from the cost of certain stocks bought in their province.

Preferred Shares – Two Investments in One

Preferred shares are a hybrid investment offering the best – and the worst – of both the equity and debt worlds.

Preferred shareholders, like common shareholders, are part owners of the company whose stock they hold, but they normally have no vote in firm affairs. Like debt instruments such as bonds and debentures, preferreds are fixed-income securities, offering a fixed dividend out of net earnings. Since they don't benefit directly from a company's increased profits, they don't offer the same potential for capital gain as do common shares, and their price doesn't normally fluctuate on the market as much as the common stock might.

Dividends are Optional

Dividends on preferred shares are not a legal requirement.

However, unlike debt interest, dividends are not a legal requirement. Dividends are paid from current or past earnings. If the directors decide to omit the payment of a preferred dividend – perhaps to preserve working capital in an emergency – there's little the preferred shareholders can do about it. Normally, however, no dividends are paid to common shareholders until preferred shareholders have received full payment of dividends to which they are entitled.

Thus, the preferred shareholder occupies a position between that of the common shareholder and that of the company's creditors. If the firm's ability to pay interest and dividends deteriorates because of lower earnings, the preferred shareholder is better protected than the common shareholders but junior to the claims of the debt holders.

Similarly, if the firm is wound up or dissolved, preferred shareholders line up behind the creditors and debt-holders. At the end of the line is the common shareholder, who has to be content with anything that is left after all creditor, debt-holder and preferred shareholder claims have been met.

Why Companies Issue Preferred Shares

In deciding which type of security to issue – preferred or common shares, or debt – there are several factors a firm would consider. Since the greatest similarities are between preferreds and debt, that's probably where the choice would lie. Companies normally find issuing preferred shares a more expensive way to raise capital, compared to bonds or debentures. The reason is that interest paid on debt instruments is a tax-deductible expense, because interest is considered a legitimate cost of doing business. Dividends, on the other hand, are a distribution of company profits. As a result they are not tax-deductible and are paid with more costly after-tax dollars.

Nonetheless, circumstances sometimes do justify a new preferred share issue. First, from the firm's viewpoint, straight preferreds do not create the demands that a debt issue creates. With preferreds there is no maturity date, which may come at a financially awkward time. If the firm's directors need to omit a preferred dividend, they can do so without jeopardizing the company's solvency. If interest isn't paid when due on debt issues, the bond or debenture holders have recourse to seizing assets. This isn't an option open to preferred shareholders denied their dividend.

Also, there are times when it simply isn't feasible to market a new debt issue. Perhaps the market is temporarily unreceptive to new debt issues. The firm may already have a lot of debt outstanding, and preferreds are issued to add balance to the capital structure and to increase the equity base. Or the company's existing assets may be heavily mortgaged already; or it may operate in a business that has few assets available for pledging, like a sales finance company. Finally, a firm may have a low apparent tax rate, which means less of a burden to pay dividends from after-tax profits.

Second, when a company has decided it will not or cannot issue bonds or debentures, it may find conditions unfavorable for selling common shares. The stock market may be falling or inactive, or business prospects may be uncertain. However, in such circumstances preferred shares might be marketed as a compromise acceptable to both the issuing company and investors. Straight preferreds also offer the advantage of avoiding the dilution of equity that results from a new issue of common shares.

Why Investors Buy Preferred Shares

Conservative investors seeking income buy preferred shares, in part to take advantage of the Dividend Tax Credit. The system of taxation for dividends results in less tax being paid on dividend income than on an equivalent amount of interest income. The tax system recognizes, at least partly, that since dividends are paid out of company profits, they have already been taxed before being paid to shareholders.

Preferred shares are also bought as an income investment by Canadian companies, because dividends paid by one resident taxable Canadian company to a similar firm are not taxable in the hands of the receiving company. This isn't the case with debt interest. When Canadian Company One buys a debt issue of

Canadian Company Two, the interest received by Company One is fully taxable in Company One's hands.

Dividend Tax Credit

Assume an investor in a 24% federal tax bracket receives $1,000 in dividends.

1. Gross up dividend by 25%	$1,000 + 250 + 1,250
2. Calculate federal tax	24% of 1,250 = 300
3. Calculate dividend tax credit	13.33% of 1,250 = 167
4. Calculate federal tax payable	300 - 167 = 133

Like common shares, preferreds can be listed on a stock exchange or traded over-the-counter.

Features of Preferred Shares

The description of the rights of a preferred shareholder is found in the charter of the company. A firm wishing to issue preferred shares must apply to make the necessary changes to its charter, unless the existing charter provides for issuance of preferred shares at the discretion of the directors.

A variety of features can be built into all types of preferred shares. Some features strengthen the issuer's position; others protect the purchaser's position. The ultimate combination of features in a new issue usually represents a compromise that will safeguard the interests of the buyer without unduly restricting the issuer.

If you want to get more information on the features of a particular preferred share, your broker or investment advisor should be able to help. You can also do your own research through the Financial Post Historical Report for that company, or special annual "Survey" books such as the Financial Post Survey of Industrials.

Cumulative and Non-cumulative

Most Canadian preferred shares have a cumulative feature built into their terms. If a firm's financial condition weakens because of a decline in earnings, the directors may reluctantly decide to omit a preferred dividend. The unpaid dividends accumulate or pile up in what is known as arrears.

Now, most people wouldn't be interested in buying a preferred that wasn't paying its dividend, and a decision not to pay a dividend will cause the market price of the preferred shares to decline as investors flee the stock. The shares assume a speculative aspect, which will become more pronounced if subsequent dividends are passed, and arrears continue to accumulate. Later, if the company's earnings improve or if losses change to profit, some investors may buy the preferred on speculation that dividends will resume. But it's not a sure bet because all arrears of cumulative preferred dividends must be paid before common dividends are paid or before the preferred shares are redeemed.

If a partial or complete repayment of arrears does materialize, however, the gains can be substantial. Payment is made to the preferred shareholders owning stock at time of repayment. Imagine, for example, that you had bought a preferred at $7.50 with $2.50 of dividend arrears. If payments resume, you have made a 33% return, and the price of the preferred will also increase. No payments are made to preferred shareholders who previously sold their stock and no interest is paid on arrears.

Few Canadian preferred shares are non-cumulative, where the shareholder is entitled to payment of a specified dividend in any year only when declared. When a non-cumulative preferred dividend is passed, arrears do not accrue and the preferred shareholder isn't entitled to "catch-up" payments if dividends resume. For this reason the dividend position of non-cumulative preferred shares is weak.

Callable and Non-callable

A call feature is a convenience to the issuer, not normally an advantage to the purchaser.

Issuers of preferred shares often reserve the right to call or redeem preferred issues. A call feature is a convenience to the issuer, not normally an advantage to the purchaser.

As with callable corporate debt, callable preferreds usually provide for payment of a small premium above the amount of per share asset entitlement fixed by the charter, as compensation to the investor whose shares are being called in. Accepted practice is for the issuer to give 30 days' notice of intention to redeem.

It's usual to give the issuing company the privilege of buying shares for cancellation on the open market or through invitations for tenders addressed to all holders. The price paid under these circumstances generally must not exceed the par value of the preferred shares plus the premium provided for redemption by call.

Non-callable preferred shares cannot be called or redeemed. This feature is restrictive from the issuer's standpoint, in that it freezes a part of its capital structure for the life of the issue. For that reason, the non-callable feature is rarely built into the terms of Canadian preferreds.

Voting Privileges

Preferred shares are non-voting so long as preferred dividends are paid on schedule.

Virtually all preferred shares are non-voting so long as preferred dividends are paid on schedule. If they aren't, it's common practice to assign voting privileges to the preferred once a stated number of dividends have been omitted. Issuing companies consider a non-voting feature advantageous, since it usually ensures the preferred shareholders have no say in running the firm's affairs.

Nonetheless, preferred shareholders are usually given a vote on matters affecting the quality of their security – for example, increasing the amount of preferred stock authorized. Sometimes, preferred shareholder approval is obtained before a debt issue is created.

Purchase Funds and Sinking Funds

Many redeemable Canadian preferred shares have a purchase fund built into their terms. With this feature, the firm agrees to retire, through purchases in the open market, a specified amount of preferred shares each year if stock is available at or below a stipulated price. However, if the purchase fund isn't able to buy enough shares in the open market, no redemption is done.

A purchase fund is advantageous to preferred shareholders

because it means that if the price of the shares declines in the market below a certain level, the fund will make every effort to buy specified amounts of shares for redemption. As a result, this type of issue has potential built-in market support.

Special Protective Provisions

Underwriters encourage companies creating new preferreds to build in specified protective provisions to safeguard the position of the preferred shareholder and make the issue more saleable. Here is a list of some of the more common provisions:

- restrictions on common dividends if they weaken the firm's financial position;
- the right to vote if dividends are in arrears;
- restrictions on further preferred issues;
- restrictions on asset sales;
- restrictions on changing the terms of the preferred.

Types of Preferred Shares

In addition to these protective provisions and the size of the dividend, there are several other special features that characterize the most common types of preferred shares.

Straight Preferreds

To begin with, those with no special features are called straight preferreds. These are preferred shares with normal preferences as to asset and dividend entitlement ahead of the common shares. Straight preferreds may have any or all of the special features described earlier. Since straight preferreds pay a fixed rate of dividends, the shares trade in the market on a yield basis. As with the market price of bonds and debentures, if interest rates rise, the market price of straight preferreds will fall and if interest rates decline their price will rise.

Straight preferreds usually have no special features.

Convertible Preferreds – Valued Flexibility for Investors

Convertible preferreds can be converted into some other class of shares.

Convertible preferreds, on the other hand, are similar to convertible bonds and debentures because they enable you to convert the preferred into some other class of shares, usually common, at a predetermined price and for a stated period.

Conversion terms are set when the preferred is created and normally the conversion price is set at a modest premium, perhaps 10% – 15% above the then prevailing market for the common. The purpose of the premium is to discourage an early conversion, which would defeat the purpose of the convertible offering. Virtually all conversion privileges expire after a stated period, usually five to twelve years from date of issue. Conversion terms may include conversion price changes at predetermined times.

If the common shares rise in price above the preferred's conversion price, the market price of the convertible preferred will rise accordingly. When this occurs, the preferred is described as selling off the common stock and the market action of the preferred will reflect the market action of the common. During this time the convertible preferred will usually sell at a premium above the price it might be expected to sell at, based on the conversion terms.

Once a convertible preferred is exercised it's not possible to convert back. No commission is charged on conversion and no capital gain or capital loss is incurred until the subsequent sale of shares received from conversion.

If the underlying common shares are split, the conversion terms are adjusted automatically on the basis of the larger number of new underlying shares.

You might be wondering why a company would issue a convertible preferred. After all, it gives the decision to convert exclusively to the investor, exposes the firm to selling common shares for less than market value, and reduces the issuer's control over the proportionate mix of common and preferred shares in its capital structure.

Why Companies Issue Convertibles

The reason is that there are sometimes circumstances in which a straight preferred is difficult to sell or situations where a high level of dividend coverage is lacking. Because a conversion feature is popular with investors, the dividend can be less than that of a comparable straight preferred and the convertible preferred can still be saleable.

Convertible preferreds are popular with investors.

Most convertible preferreds are redeemable, which gives the issuer the power to force a conversion into the underlying shares when the market price of the preferred rises above the redemption price. To force a conversion, management announces the redemption of the preferred at the call price as at a certain date. Convertible preferred shareholders convert their shares because of the price advantage. A forced conversion is done only if management decides there's an advantage to retiring the preferred by issuing new common shares.

Retractable Preferreds

While most preferred shares are redeemable, it's up to the issuer whether redemption actually occurs. As a retractable preferred shareholder, on the other hand, you can force the firm to redeem

---

Retractable Preferred Shares

- **provide a predetermined date(s) and price(s) to tender shares for retraction – the shorter the time interval to the retraction date, the less vulnerable is the stock's market price to increases in interest rates**
- **provide a capital gain if purchases at a discount from the retraction price and subsequent tendered at the retraction price**
- **will sell above the retraction price and at least as high as the redemption price if interest rates decline sufficiently**
- **do not automatically redeem – if no action is taken by the holder during the election period(s), the retraction privilege will expire**
- **become straight preferred shares if not retracted when the election period expires**
- **revert to a straight preferred when the conversion period expires**

---

the retractable preferred on a specified date and at a specified price. You can create a maturity date for the preferred by exercising the retraction privilege and tendering the shares to the issuer for redemption.

Variable or Floating Rate Preferreds

Identical in concept to variable or floating rate debentures, variable rate preferreds pay dividends in amounts that fluctuate to reflect changes in interest rates. If interest rates rise, so will dividend payments and vice versa.

Variable rate preferreds are issued during periods in the market when a straight preferred is hard to sell and the issuer has rejected making the issue convertible, because of potential dilution of common equity, or retractable, because holders could force redemption on a specified date. The issuer usually believes interest rates will not go much higher, but in any event is prepared to pay a higher dividend if interest rates rise. Of course, if interest rates decline, the issuer will pay a smaller dividend, subject in most

---

Variable Rate Preferreds

- **the dividend payout is tied to changes in interest rates on a predetermined basis**
- **provide higher income if interest rates rise, but lower income if interest rates fall**
- **provide a variable amount of annual income which is difficult to predict accurately but which will reflect prevailing interest rate levels**
- **provide an investment with a market price less responsive to changes in interest rates vis-a-vis the market prices of straight preferred shares**

Participating Preferred Shares

- **provide the possibility of higher dividend income when the company's earnings permit**
- **provide only a marginal advantage over the common shares if a limited participation feature is present**

---

cases to a guaranteed minimum rate.

Some preferred shares may have delayed variable rate features. Known as delayed floaters or fixed floaters, these shares entitle the holder to a fixed dividend for a predetermined period, after which the dividend becomes variable.

Participating Preferreds

Participating preferred shares have certain rights to a share in the earnings of the company over and above their specified dividend rate.

Foreign-pay Preferreds

Most Canadian preferreds pay dividends in Canadian funds. However, it's possible for a company to create and issue preferreds with dividends and certain other features payable in or related to foreign funds. The key factor to selecting such a preferred is the desirability of getting dividends in a currency other than Canadian funds. You benefit if the foreign currency rises against the Canadian dollar. If the foreign currency falls against the Canadian dollar, you'll wish you had stuck to a straight preferred.

Rights and Warrants

Sometimes when a firm wants to raise more money it will issue rights and/or warrants. These allow the shareholder to buy more shares directly from the company, usually at a price somewhat lower than the current market price of the old shares. This is a way for a firm to raise more funds in a way that favours existing shareholders.

The major difference between rights and warrants is their lifespan. Rights usually expire after a few weeks, while warrants can continue from one to several years. Both can trade on the market separately from the company's stock.

The customary method of making a rights offering is to issue one right for each common share outstanding. You can then combine the rights into the multiples required for one or more shares and subscribe. No commission is levied when you exercise the rights and acquire new shares. Normally fractional shares are not issued.

A ready market in the rights usually develops, permitting surplus rights to be sold or more rights to be bought. The possibility that the market price of the stock will fall below the subscription price is of major importance in setting the terms of a rights issue. If this happened, you wouldn't exercise your rights and the share issue would fail. To minimize this risk, many rights issues are underwritten by an investment dealer. In return for a fee, the underwriter will generally stand ready to purchase a certain number of the unsubscribed shares for at least the subscription price.

Intrinsic and Time Value of Rights and Warrants

The value of a right closely resembles the difference between its subscription price and the market price of the stock. This amount is the right's intrinsic value. If the right is trading for more than its intrinsic value, we call the extra amount its time value. Once rights expire they are worthless and may not be exercised.

A warrant is often attached to new debt and preferred issues to make these issues more attractive to buyers, thereby functioning as a sweetener.

Intrinsic Value = stock price - subscription price.

Time Value = right price - intrinsic value.

Right Price = intrinsic value + time value.

Like rights, warrants may have an intrinsic value and a time value. Intrinsic value is the amount by which the market price of the underlying common stock exceeds the subscription price (also known as the excercise price of the warrant.)

A warrant has no intrinsic value if the exercise price is above the current market value of the shares; however, it will still usually have a market value known as time value because of perceived speculative potential up to the expiry date.

Leverage – The Main Attraction of Warrants

The main speculative attraction of warrants is their leverage potential. The price of a warrant is usually much less than the price of the underlying security and generally moves together with it. The capital appreciation of a warrant on a percentage basis can therefore greatly exceed that of the underlying security. This chart illustrates the idea of leverage. Assume there is a warrant with a market value of $4, exercisable at $12 on an underlying common stock whose market price is $15. If the common rises to $23 before the warrants expire, the warrants would rise to at least their intrinsic value of $11 (23 – 12), an increase of 175% of the original outlay. The common shares would have appreciated only 53%.

Of course, the reverse is also true. A fall in the price of the common from $15 to $11 results in a 27% loss in share value compared with a potential 100% loss in the value of the warrant, assuming again that it has no time value.

Warrant exercisable at $12

	Stock at 15	Stock at 23	Stock at 11
Warrant Price	4	11	0
Intrinsic Value	3	11	0
Time Value	1	0	0
Stock $ Gain (Loss)		8	(4)
Stock % Gain (Loss)		53	(27)
Warrant $ Gain (Loss)		7	(4)
Warrant % Gain (Loss)		175	(100)

Deciding Where to Put your Money

Choosing the correct investment from among a wide variety of places to put your money is the most difficult job in investing. However, many people contemplating buying securities for the first time are too busy to get the necessary background and information to make these decisions on their own. To reduce avoidable mistakes, novice investors should seek the advice of a reputable securities firm or investment advisor before making an initial purchase of securities. While competent advice is key, it isn't an end in itself. The successful investor continually seeks more knowledge about the securities markets.

Gone are the days when an investor could rely on a stock tip overheard at a cocktail party! Information travels too fast these days, and that hot tip is most likely old news by the time you hear it. Still, you shouldn't ignore all of your hunches when looking for a ripe stock. Let's say you hear that that discount electronics retailer up the street plans an initial public offering of stock. Last time you were in the store, it seemed to be doing a booming business. Maybe this firm deserves a closer look as a possible investment.

Another source for investment tips is brokers' research reports. But unless you plan to put money into everything that has a "buy" recommendation attached to it, you'll have to be able to make sense of the report by knowing the language it uses.

Different Ways to Evaluate Stock

What makes one stock worth buying over another? There are many different ways to judge a stock's merits. Strong profit performance is key. But this might already be reflected in the firm's stock price, and the shares could already have run out of steam. Only a careful analysis will indicate whether a stock has further upside, based on forecasts for future earnings. This approach, which makes use of the price-to-earnings (or P/E) ratio, will be discussed in greater detail later.

Besides earnings, many analysts will focus on a company's balance sheet, where assets are matched against liabilities. By dividing the firm's net asset value by the number of its shares outstanding, the analyst can learn whether the stock is undervalued or overvalued in the market relative to other companies in the same line of business.

Alternatively, a stock can be rated in the context of the economy. If interest rates are on a downswing, this would favor interest-sensitive stocks like banks and utilities. By the same token, once an economic recovery takes hold and corporate earnings are heading higher, manufacturing and resource stocks would benefit.

Then there's simply the phenomenon of a hot stock. These Holy Grails of the stock market are so exceptional that they will outperform the market, regardless of the state of the economy or the particular industry. Finding these gems, however, requires a lot of skill, or luck, or both.

Still another way of evaluating stocks is technical analysis, which largely ignores the fundamental details of a company's sales and profits. Instead, the technical analyst may chart past trends in the movement of the firm's stock price and in trading volumes to time the next significant move up or down in the shares. From these charts, the analyst expects to be able to spot heavy demand, indicating an up trend in the stock, or sudden supply, suggesting a downtrend.

Here's an example of how technical analysis works. It's assumed that the news of a favorable development related to a firm tends to spread from group to group in waves. First one group of people will buy the stock, and its price will go up on heavy volume. Then there will be a quiet period and the stock will sell off. After a while a new group of people will hear the news and buy the stock, and again it will go up on heavy volume. When technical analysts spot this pattern on a chart, they are alerted to the buying, and probably will favor the stock.

Which Method is Most Reliable?

As you might expect, investors often wonder which method of evaluating a stock will prove the most reliable. The answer is all of them, and none of them alone. Statistical analysis, which examines such things as the P/E ratio, or the net asset value per share, is helpful but must be used with caution. One ratio alone doesn't tell much. Ratios are not proofs, but clues to a judgment. Also, the significance of a ratio may vary between different types of companies in different industries. We'll talk more about financial ratios later.

Analysis by Industry Type

As a first step in fundamental analysis, it's common practice to select industries that are likely to perform best during a given period – say 12 to 24 months – and then to select individual companies likely to lead those industries. To identify the best companies for investment, we need to have a sense of how industries evolve, and what this means for stock prices. Broadly speaking, there are a few recognizable stages in an industry's evolution.

Emerging Industries

The value of many of the companies in emerging industries is not based on traditional benchmarks but on the potential of a good idea.

These develop new products or services to meet society's needs and demands. The transportation industry, for example, has gone from horse-drawn carriages to supersonic airplanes in a few decades. Today, the pace of change continues to accelerate, creating more investment opportunities than ever. Rapid innovation in personal computing technology and telecommunications, for example, has set the stage for the explosive growth of Web-based commerce. Typically, the value of many of these companies is based not on traditional benchmarks such as P/E ratios but on the potential of a good idea. In fact, many Web-based companies have impressive market capitalizations despite the fact they have yet to turn a profit.

Growth Industries

These typically have sales and earnings that are consistently expanding at a faster rate than most industries. Such companies are called growth companies and their shares are growth stocks. Growth stocks generally have increased in value at well above average rates for at least five years, and are expected to continue to do so. A mere rise in price doesn't make a growth stock. Instead, the rise must be based on permanent factors, such as increasing sales, earnings and value of assets.

Growth stocks usually have the following characteristics:

- a high rate of earnings on invested capital;

- retention and reinvestment of earnings, rather than paying much of this out in dividends;
- capable and aggressive management; and
- fertile opportunity for earnings growth.

Current examples of growth industries include computer software, telecommunications equipment and biotechnology.

Stable Industries

These have sales and earnings that are stable and tend to hold up even in a recession. This stability, however, doesn't guarantee immunity from the downward momentum of a bear market, although price swings may be moderate. Such companies usually have the internal resources to weather difficult economic conditions successfully.

Companies in stable industries tend to fit into three main categories:

- Blue chip stocks are top investment quality companies that maintain earnings and dividends through good times and bad. They often show strong growth in sales and earnings, but are different from growth companies in that they are larger, have a certain market dominance and are more seasoned. Still, a blue chip stock offers no guarantee of continued performance, as company fortunes can and do change. Many investors consider Canada's major chartered banks to be blue chips.
- Defensive stocks are somewhat immune to poor economic conditions. Utilities are an example in this group, because of the essential and continuing services they provide. Other industries in which sales hold up well even in economic downturns include brewing, pharmaceuticals and food wholesaling. However, other factors need to be considered when investing in these industries, such as price competition within the industry.
- Income stocks provide a generous dividend yield that is reasonably assured. At the same time, this attractive yield might imply a reasonably low degree of price volatility and limited

potential for capital appreciation. Shares of utility companies are also classified as income stocks, as well as blue chip and defensive stocks.

Be aware that not all stocks with high dividend yields are income stocks. For example, a high current yield may be the result of a large drop in the stock's price in anticipation of possible financial difficulties at the firm.

Cyclical Industries

These include companies with earnings that are particularly sensitive to the business cycle. Few, if any, industries are immune from the adverse effects of an overall business downturn, but the term cyclical applies to those for which the effect on earnings is most pronounced. As business conditions improve, earnings tend to rebound dramatically. Examples of cyclical industries include steel, forest products, cement, automobiles, household appliances and heavy equipment.

Some companies are affected by seasonal factors, but this doesn't make them cyclical stocks. Brewing companies, for instance, have higher sales in the summer, but are reasonably stable year to year.

Speculative Industries

These involve higher risk than normal equity investments, because of an absence of definitive information. Emerging industries, for instance, can be called speculative; there's no assurance that a particular firm will be among the survivors that enjoy the benefit of a new technology. In Canada, speculative often refers to the so-called penny stocks, mainly junior mining and oil and gas ventures. The term speculative is also used when a growth company's stock is bid up sharply on an expectation of continuing exceptional growth. If these expectations suddenly deflate for some reason, the stock could plunge.

Declining Industries

These involve products for which demand is in decline because of changes in technology or consumer preference. However, companies in these situations can survive by diversifying operations or by acquiring other companies, if management takes appropriate action at an early stage. Steel manufacturing is an example of a declining industry. Many of the uses for steel have been supplanted by plastic compounds or other materials.

Evaluating Different Industries

For the investor with a high risk tolerance, emerging industries and growth stocks offer the biggest potential return on investment. But for most people, a diversified portfolio of securities with a highly volatile stock balanced out by a stable defensive stock is preferable. Although this type of portfolio's overall return might be lower, there's less chance of losing the farm.

Evaluating stocks by industry also helps the analyst keep track of factors that affect all the companies in an industry. For example, swings in world commodity prices will affect most mining stocks, although some will be affected more than others. And most financial services companies are likely to feel the effects of a change in interest rates.

Reading the business section of a daily newspaper will help you catch some of this kind of information. Also, weekly or monthly business magazines usually have more in-depth articles on companies and the challenges they are facing. And investment newsletters usually try to provide the specific information that is critical to making an investment decision.

Although an informed investor wants to know when there's a change in the price of a commodity, such as lumber, it's probably too late at that point to buy those stocks. Cyclical stocks usually go up in anticipation of stronger commodity prices, not after the fact. So reading analysts' research reports, distributed by the various brokerage houses to their clients, could keep you informed of events that are expected to develop in the near future. Some of these forecasts are also reported in business newspapers.

Once you have identified an industry of interest, the next step is to look at the specific companies within that sector. Your analysis should then lead to a comparative evaluation of all major companies in that industry. Each firm will be unique in the way it does business and finances its operations.

Choosing a Company

Quantitative analysis draws heavily on data from published financial statements.

Company analysis has two parts: quantitative analysis, which draws heavily on data from published financial statements; and qualitative analysis, which attempts to assess intangible factors such as the quality of management. For both the professional analyst and the novice investor, a valuable source of information on a firm is its annual report to shareholders, which usually can be obtained by phoning the company. In addition, most annual reports can be downloaded from the company's Web site or through regulatory agencies.

The average investor with little or no training in accounting usually finds it difficult to make sense of company financial statements. However, with just a little time invested, these statements are not hard to understand and interpret. They can reveal a great deal about a firm's financial health.

Qualitative analysis attempts to assess intangible factors such as the quality of manage-ment.

Buying a company's shares amounts to an investment in its future prospects, which are difficult to forecast with accuracy. But the past often provides a clue to the future, and if you have some knowledge of a company's present financial position and its past earnings record, you are more likely to select securities that will stand the test of time. As we discussed, you'll need to combine this information with an understanding of the industry in which the company operates, the economy generally, and the specific plans and prospects for the company in question to make a sound selection from your investment alternatives.

Besides providing a company's financial statements, the typical annual report contains other valuable information. Some companies are more forthcoming in their annual reports than others. An important section to read is the president's report to shareholders, which covers highlights of the past year, comments on the outlook for the current year and discusses such items as expansion plans, management and product changes. Make sure you read the management discussion and analysis section. The annual report also may include comparative operating and financial statistics for the past five or ten years, information on the various segments of the company's business, graphs and pictures of the company's plants, products and services.

Assets: what the company owns

Liabilities: what the company owes

Owner's Equity: the worth or the value of the company

Assets = Liabilities + Owner's Equity

Measuring Performance with Financial Statements

The core of the annual report is the balance sheet and earnings statement. The balance sheet breaks down the company's assets and offsetting liabilities, with the difference being the equity value of the company, which is owned by the shareholders.

The Earnings Statement

The earnings statement shows how much revenue a company received during the year from the sale of its products or services and the expenses it incurred for wages, materials, operating costs, taxes and other expenses. The difference between the revenue and expenses is the company's profit or loss for the year.

Net Income = Revenue - Expenses

Earnings per common share $= \dfrac{\textbf{net earnings - any preferred dividends}}{\textbf{number of common shares outstanding}}$

Retained earnings = net income = any dividends

An important number from the shareholder's point of view is earnings per share, which is derived from the earnings statement. By expressing a company's net earnings in this way, the shareholder is able to see clearly how profitable their ownership interest in the company is and whether dividends are likely to be paid.

The only direct link between the earnings statement and the balance sheet is through what is called retained earnings. After a company figures its net profit, the so-called bottom line, it may pay a dividend to its shareholders. Any profit then left over is retained by the company and is added to the shareholders' equity on the balance sheet.

Sales

When assessing the outlook for a company's profitability, the first thing to consider is its ability to increase sales. Whether sales are increasing or decreasing, the trend should be analyzed to isolate the main causes. For example, a rising trend may reflect such factors as increases in product prices or product volumes, the acquisition of a new company or a gain in market share, or an upswing in the business cycle. By isolating the main factors affecting sales, you are better able to judge whether the trend will continue into the future.

Operating Costs

The next step is to look at operating costs to assess the overall efficiency of operations. Just because operating costs go up doesn't mean a company is in trouble; it's normal for these costs to rise as sales increase. What's key is whether operating costs as a percentage of sales is rising, stable or declining. A rising trend over several years may indicate that a company is having difficulty keeping overall costs under control, which would hurt its profitability. A falling trend suggests that a company is becoming more cost effective, which should help profits.

Again, it's key to consider the main reasons for changes in operating costs. Although these may be difficult to find out, they are important in understanding what affects the company's cost structure. Factors that can affect operating costs include the cost of raw materials, the introduction of more efficient equipment, or an increase in wage payments.

After-tax Profit

Finally, toward the bottom of the earnings statement is the company's net after-tax profit or loss. Regardless of whether this is up or down in the latest year, what matters is the trend over several years. One way to assess this trend is by comparing the net profit as a percentage of sales, called the net profit margin, over several years. This provides a quick reference to the ability of management to produce profits.

Return on Equity

Analysts also use several other financial ratios to judge how well management makes use of a company's resources. One common ratio is the return on equity, which indicates management's effectiveness at increasing profitability in relation to the equity capital of the company. A declining trend reveals for shareholders that their investment is being employed less productively.

Inventory Turnover

Another measure of efficiency, and thus profitability, is the inventory turnover ratio, which is important for companies that carry substantial inventories, such as manufacturers and merchandisers. The ratio measures the number of times a company's inventory is turned over in a year. It may also be expressed as a number of days. A high turnover ratio is considered desirable, because this requires a smaller investment in inventory than a company that produces the same sales with a low turnover. There is no standard yardstick for this ratio, as inventory turnover rates vary greatly from industry to industry.

$$\textbf{Net profit margin} = \frac{\textbf{net income - equity income + minority interest}}{\textbf{net sales}}$$

$$\textbf{Net return on equity} = \frac{\textbf{net income - preferred dividends (if any)}}{\textbf{common equity}}$$

$$\textbf{Inventory turnover ratio} = \frac{\textbf{cost of goods sold}}{\textbf{inventory}}$$

Growth versus Value Investing

Growth investors focus on a company's potential to generate superior earnings.

Investors who focus on a company's potential to generate superior earnings are known as growth investors. As future earnings grow, goes the reasoning, so will the company's share price. Other investors, instead, look for value when buying a stock. In effect, they ask: is the market pricing a particular stock too cheaply? This value can be measured in several ways. Usually when we think of securities having yields we think of interest rates on bonds. But stocks have yields too, based on their dividend payouts, expressed as a percentage of the share price. Dividend yields represent the investor's percentage return on an investment at its prevailing market price, and enable the investor at least superficially to compare shares of different companies. The problem is that dividend yields don't reveal some important aspects of a company, such as the quality and record of its management. Or what percentage of earnings is being retained to take advantage of more growth opportunities. Also, it's important to remember that some stocks have high dividend yields because the share price has dropped off, perhaps for good reason.

Price to Earnings Ratio

$$\text{current yield} = \frac{\text{annual dividend}}{\text{current market price}} \times 100$$

$$\text{P/E} = \frac{\text{current market price}}{\text{earnings per share}}$$

Probably the most widely used measure of a stock's value is the price-to-earnings, or P/E, ratio. This provides a comparison between different stocks by creating a ratio of the market price of each stock relative to its earnings per share. The P/E ratio, which is only calculated for common shares, is a useful measurement because it reflects the views of thousands of investors on the issue's quality. However, P/E ratios of different stocks can only be compared when the companies are in the same line of business; each industry tends to have its own P/E ratio level that is considered normal. But even this norm can change, rising usually when the overall market is going up, and falling when the market is in retreat.

Value investors look for low P/E ratios, which could signal that a stock is undervalued by the market. Growth investors, on the other hand, are more comfortable with high P/E ratios, because they expect a company's earnings will grow at a fast enough rate to justify paying a high market price. There is no standard P/E ratio. Still, we can safely say that stable industries such as banks and utilities tend to have low P/E ratios, whereas more speculative investments such as gold mining, communication and Internet stocks would have higher ratios.

Value investors look for low P/E ratios, which could signal that a stock is undervalued by the market.

The Balance Sheet

Now that we've discussed how analysts use a company's earnings statement to evaluate its stock, let's look at what a typical balance sheet can reveal to the potential investor. Companies sell shares to the public to finance their business operations. Many companies also issue debt securities and take out bank loans to further expand their operations and add flexibility to their financing. A careful investor will keep a close eye on the amount and type of debt a company has in order to assess its financial health. A company with too much debt runs the risk of having its profits eaten away by interest charges when business slows down. On the other hand, having too little debt is seen as not making efficient use of the company's assets, with the result that profits are lower than they could be. To find out how much debt is too much debt, you should start with a careful analysis of a company's balance sheet.

A Balance Sheet has Three Main Sections

On one side of the balance sheet are listed the company's assets, including current assets, such as inventories, which can be turned into cash quite easily. Then there are fixed assets, usually buildings and machinery not intended to be sold.

These and various other asset categories are offset by the company's liabilities, which are listed on the other side of the balance sheet. Included here are current liabilities, which are

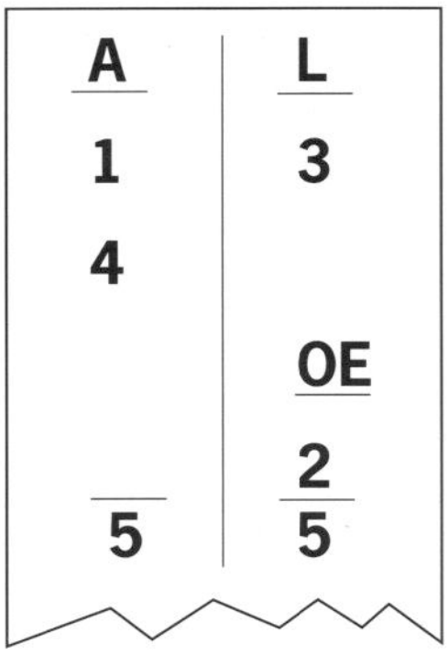

A	L
1	3
4	
	OE
	2
5	5

debts due within a year or those that a company incurs in the ordinary course of doing business, such as unpaid bills. Another liability is long-term debts, which come due more than a year in the future. Typical long-term debts are mortgages, bonds and debentures.

As we mentioned, the difference between a company's assets and its liabilities is the equity value of the company that is owned by the shareholders. The Shareholders' Equity section of the balance sheet usually appears under the Liabilities, so that one side of the balance sheet equals the other.

The Importance of Liquidity

An important piece of information you can gain by reviewing the balance sheet is the extent of a company's liquidity, or its ability to access funds readily.

Liquidity is something every company needs to meet its obligations, expand its volume of business and take advantage of financial opportunities. A lack of liquidity is a frequent cause of business failure.

Working Capital Ratio

A company's liquid assets are referred to as working capital, which is simply the difference between the current assets and current liabilities on the balance sheet. As an analytical tool, however, the investor is interested in a calculation known as the working capital ratio. This is arrived at by dividing a company's current assets by its current liabilities. A ratio of 2:1, for example, reveals that a company has $2 in current assets to pay for each $1 of current liabilities. As a rule of thumb, a 2:1 working capital ratio is considered a minimum, although this can vary, depending on the type of business. Working capital ratios can also be too high. A ratio that consistently runs above 5:1 could indicate the company has excess inventory that it can't sell, or perhaps that its management is overly cautious.

The Quick Ratio

A more stringent gauge of a company's liquidity is known as the quick ratio, or the acid test. In this test, a company's inventories, which are sometimes difficult to turn into ready cash, are excluded from current assets before doing the working capital ratio calculation. What's left in current assets is just actual cash and other quick assets, such as government treasury bills. There is no standard for this ratio, although a company is generally considered to be in a good liquidity position if it has at least $1 in quick assets for every $1 in current liabilities. However, some companies may be just fine with a quick asset ratio of less than one-to-one if they have a high rate of inventory turnover.

$$\textbf{working capital or current ratio} = \frac{\textbf{current assets}}{\textbf{current liabilities}}$$

$$\textbf{quick ratio} = \frac{\textbf{current assets - inventories}}{\textbf{current liabilities}}$$

Debt to Total Capitalization

Even if a company passes these measures of liquidity, it's still possible that it has too much debt to pay back. To find out if that's the case, you need to look at a company's debt in relation to its total capitalization. As we discussed, a company gets its capital from various sources, including retained earnings, common shareholders, preferred shareholders – which are all part of Shareholder's Equity – and bank loans and other debt instruments. The conscientious investor wants to know how much of a company's total capitalization can be made up of debt without setting off warning bells.

$$\textbf{\% of debt in capital structure} = \frac{\textbf{total debt}}{\textbf{total debt + equity}} \times 100$$

Unfortunately, there's no easy answer for this. The relationship of debt to total capitalization varies widely for companies in different industries. For example, it's normal for public utility, pipeline and real estate companies to have a big proportion of their capital structure made up of debt. But if a company that manufactures products subject to wide fluctuation in demand has as much debt in its capital structure as does a public utility, the soundness of its capital structure would be questioned. Analysts use a certain amount of intuition in judging what is acceptable capitalization. But as a rule of thumb, industrial companies' capital should be limited to at most one-third debt.

Debt to Equity Ratio

Another way of looking at levels of debt is through the debt-to-equity ratio. As its name implies, this test measures a company's total debt as a proportion of shareholders' equity. This is a key measure that can serve as a warning that a company's borrowing is excessive; the higher the ratio, the higher the financial risk. Again there is a rule of thumb, which must be applied flexibly. Industrial companies' debt should be at most half the equity value.

$$\text{debt/equity} = \frac{\text{total debt}}{\text{shareholders' equity}}$$

Interest Coverage

$$\text{Interest Coverage} = \frac{\text{net income - equity income + minority interest + taxes + all interst charges}}{\text{all interest charges}}$$

Finally, let's see how we can evaluate a company's ability to service its debt, that is, pay the annual interest costs. This ratio, known as interest coverage, indicates how many times the interest charges or expenses are covered by earnings available to pay them. Again, there's no single correct answer. The proper coverage varies from industry to industry, and from company to company, depending on their past earnings records and future prospects. Generally, however, an industrial company's interest charges should be covered at least three times over by the earnings available to pay them. It's important that interest coverage is consistently above minimum levels. You should examine this coverage for each of a company's preceding five years.

No matter how carefully you analyze a stock, there's always a risk that something inside the company, in the economy or in the political world could derail the best-laid investment plans. There are certain strategies that can be used to help minimize such risks, especially for a first-time investor.

The Importance of Diversification

The first is, don't put all your eggs in one basket: diversify your stock holdings. Let's say world oil prices plummet while you are holding stock in an energy company. Suddenly you are a lot poorer, at least on paper. But you probably wouldn't feel quite as bad if you also held shares in a company that benefited from low oil prices, such as a transportation concern. That's diversification. Even owning some bonds could offset the negative consequences of holding too narrow a selection of stocks. In the example above, bonds might be expected to rally if oil prices fall, because of reduced inflationary pressures in the economy.

Don't put all your eggs in one basket – diversify.

A problem with diversifying is that it costs more money to buy a variety of stocks than to buy shares in just one or two companies. Also, not every investor has the ability to build up a sufficiently diversified portfolio of stock holdings. It's a good idea to talk to a professional advisor about creating the right investment portfolio to suit your needs, and how much it will cost. One solution might be an investment in mutual funds, something we'll have more to say about in Chapter 6.

Dollar Cost Averaging

One thing that stymies nearly all investors at some point is picking the right time to buy or sell a stock. If you bought $5,000 worth of stocks one day and the market corrects 10% the next week, we'd say

	$ Invested	Price	Shares
Jan.	200	$10	20
Feb.	200	$8	25
March	200	$9	22.22
April	200	$12	16.67
Totals	800		83.89
Average price:		$9.75	
Average cost per share:		$9.54	

your timing was bad. How do you prevent this from happening? One way is with a discipline known as dollar cost averaging. It involves investing about the same amount at regular set intervals over a period. The funds should be invested in securities that represent reasonable value. By taking prices as they come, you sometimes pay more and sometimes less. When you pay more, you get fewer shares, since the amount invested each time is the same. So over a period of years you'll pay an average price that normally is more favorable than if you bought at random intervals.

Dollar cost averaging requires some fortitude; you must have the courage to continue buying even during market declines. Although dollar cost averaging doesn't solve the problem of what to buy, it offers a reasonable solution as to when to buy.

Keeping an Eye on Your Investments

Financial analysis doesn't stop once you choose the stocks for your portfolio. Companies should be continuously monitored for changes that might alter investment quality. One way to do this is to carefully read a company's quarterly financial statement, which is distributed to shareholders and to the financial media. Also, if a company plans to issue new shares or debt securities, it will file a prospectus with the regulatory authorities that can contain new information of material importance. Besides monitoring developments at specific companies, you should also keep abreast of general economic trends, the business cycle's anticipated direction, and various government policies that might affect investments.

The equities we've been discussing are the major source of long-term capital growth for most investors. As we will see in the following chapter, however, there are different ways to buy them and there's a whole world of derivative products based on them. Knowing about these choices will help you make better investment decisions whatever asset class you go for.

Summary

Besides borrowing money, issuing equity or shares is the other way companies raise funds. Debt and equity are the major parts of a company's capital structure. Common shares have several characteristics that appeal to investors: they carry a vote, they can appreciate in value, they can be easily bought or sold on a stock exchange or over-the-counter market, and they might pay dividends. Preferred shares do not carry a vote but they do pay a fixed dividend ahead of the common shares. Preferred shares have some characteristics in common with debt issues: they are both fixed-income investments and could have features such as sinking or purchase funds, various protective provisions, and a conversion, retraction or redemption feature.

Rights and warrants are issued by companies to allow investors to purchase shares at a stated price for a stated period. Rights are given to existing shareholders and warrants form part of a new issue of preferred shares or debentures. They both subsequently trade on stock markets. Investors will buy rights or warrants rather than the shares themselves because of the leverage potential: given a certain price increase in the stock, the right or warrant will show a greater percentage gain than the stock itself.

Much attention has been paid to evaluating and choosing stocks. Technical analysis looks at a stock's price movements to predict future trends. Fundamental analysis focuses on a company's financial position and earnings. As a starting point, it tries to identify industries with good prospects for growth, and then picks the best companies within those industries.

A company's annual report is a good source of information. Besides management reports and a breakdown of the company's operating structure, it contains the company's balance sheet and earnings statement. These statements provide the data that is needed to work out certain ratios that can be used to evaluate the company's profitability and operating efficiency. Other figures from these statements can be used to find out whether the company's shares are trading at an attractive price.

Whatever the analytic technique used, there's no guarantee that a company that scores well on the analysis will do well in reality. Diversifying investments among different companies, different types of companies, and different types of investments can soften the consequences of one poor choice. Investing the same amount in one company's shares at regular intervals, a technique known as dollar cost averaging, can solve the problem of when to buy, while lowering the average share cost.

Investment Options

A wealth of investment alternatives for those who get to know them.

Now that you know the basics of investing in stocks and bonds, it's time to take a look at another type of securities known as options. Many investors – even some veterans who have been playing the stock market for years – tend to think of options as a risky proposition. But the fact is, options can satisfy a wide range of investment goals, from leveraging your bet on the future performance of a stock to preserving income and minimizing risk.

Options and other similar securities provide knowledgeable users with alternatives. Instead of simply buying a stock, a bullish strategy, you could buy a call or a bull call spread instead; even create a synthetic long stock or synthetic long calls. Options strategies can provide you with profitable alternatives to investing in actual stocks and bonds – alternatives that are more appropriate to help you accomplish your goals.

Options and other similar securities provide knowledge-able users with alternatives.

If all this sounds complicated – it won't by the time you finish this chapter – it's to make a point. The main problem with options and similar derivative instruments is that investors don't learn enough of the basics before they jump into the market. And without that knowledge, these products can be dangerous. They can offer significant leverage to the novice investor, but leverage is a two-edged sword. You have to understand this product's power before investing.

Options have been around for a long time. Some say they were in use as a financial product as far back as ancient Egypt, although well-documented evidence of their use dates back to the tulip mania in Holland in the seventeenth century. Of course, how and where they came about really isn't the issue. The question really is: what can options do for you, the investor?

In 1634-37, a mania to possess tulips swept through Holland. When speculation crashed to a halt in 1637, it took the Dutch economy many years to get over the side effects.

The Basics of Options

There is a language that is unique to the options market. Although some terms may already be familiar to you, to fully understand and use options, you must be familiar with the proper terminology and be able to use these terms in discussing potential strategies with your investment advisor.

An option itself does not represent a tangible, physical thing in the same way a stock or bond represents ownership or money owing. An option is really just a contract or agreement between two parties – a buyer and a seller. This contract clearly specifies all the agreement's details, including what the contract is based on and how long it's to be in force. You can buy and sell these contracts just as you can buy and sell other securities.

More importantly, options can add choice and dimension to your portfolio. By purchasing an option, you can achieve a high degree of exposure with a limited and known risk level. Selling options when you own the underlying security can improve its income potential. And options also provide flexibility. By mixing and matching various options positions, you can create a vast number of strategies, to take advantage of pricing anomalies or to generate a position that reflects a complicated and personal view of the market.

Options give You Options

As the word option connotes, an option is about choice. It offers opportunities to the average investor that were never available before.

Options offer opportun-ities to the average investor that were never available before.

Say you believe the markets are overpriced and there may be a sell-off. With options, you can sell the market as represented by an index in one transaction – by purchasing an index put – in a dollar amount suitable to your own circumstances. Maybe you think the Japanese yen is going to stage a rally. Want to participate? It's as easy as buying a call on the yen. Do interest rates look like they are destined to rise? Buy puts on bonds. Now you can take advantage of your opinion to either protect your assets or to gain from your unique insights and trade an option product that will reflect your opinion.

An Option is a Contract

As mentioned earlier, an option is an agreement between two parties, the buyer and the seller. The buyer pays a fee or premium to the seller, to purchase the right to buy or sell a specific item or security. This item or security upon which the contract is based is called the underlying security or underlying interest, and can be any one of a variety of things. There are options based on equities, indexes, bonds, actual interest rates, currencies and precious metals. The option seller receives a premium and takes on the obligation of fulfilling the rights granted to the buyer. The option has a limited lifespan, called the time to expiry, which can be anywhere from one day to three years; the greater the option contract's lifespan, the greater the premium or value of the option. The expiry of an equity option occurs on the Saturday following the third Friday of the month specified in the contract. Expiration of options on other products may be at different times so you should check with your investment advisor before an order to buy an option is given.

Puts and Calls

There are two types of options: puts and calls. The put option allows the holder to sell the underlying interest, while the call option allows the holder to buy the underlying interest, either at expiration or at any time prior to the contract's expiration. If the buyer of an option decides to exercise the right to buy or sell the underlying interest or security, the transaction would be done at the price specified in the contract. This price is called the strike or exercise price.

Some options can be exercised at any time before their expiration date. Such options are called American-style or simply American options. Options listed on individual shares, or equity options, are American-style and can be exercised at any time, resulting in either the purchase or sale of the security on the day the option is exercised. Other options are European, which means they cannot be exercised until just prior to expiry. Most, but not all, index options are European-style.

What an Option Looks Like

Stocks and bonds are issued by companies to investors, and ownership is evidenced by a certificate. While most investors may never actually see a stock or bond certificate, ownership of that security is registered with the company itself. The money from the original issue of securities was received by the company to use as it saw fit.

Option writer: the creator or originator of the contract

Options, however, are not issued by the company but are derived from existing securities. That's why they are called derivative securities. The money generated by the issue of the option goes directly to its writer. The option contract between the buyer and the writer is actually issued by a third party to the transaction, the clearing corporation which was set up specifically by the exchanges that deal in options to maintain records of all listed options trading. The clearing corporation ensures that for each option buyer, there is an option seller. It guarantees the fulfillment of each contract, so there's never a risk of default once the listed option is issued to the buyer and seller. The only thing that proves ownership of an option is the contract, which is printed by the broker arranging the buy or sell, as well as the records maintained by the clearing corporation. The contract you get looks similar to this example.

Sample Only — **ABC Brokerage Ltd.**
Address

As agents, we have for your account:

Bought 5	**Opening Transaction**	**ACME**	**January 40 put @ 2.00**	**$1,000.00**
			Commission:	**50.00**
			Total:	**$1,050.00**

Account # 00-555-00 **Sales Code 15**
Tanya Lee
121 Park Street — **Transaction Date: 05-20-XX**
Big Town, Your Province — **Settlement Date: 05-21-XX**
XXX-XXX — **EXCH: XXX**

Reviewing the Options Contract

You should review the contract closely to ensure that all details are correct. Mistakes can occur and should be dealt with promptly, as options have a limited lifespan. Once they have expired, it's difficult to rectify any problems that might have occurred when the trade was done. You should retain all contracts for income tax purposes. Of particular importance to the investor are the following details listed on the contract.

(i) the type of option – put or call?

(ii) the month and strike price

(iii) the underlying security

(v) was the trade a buy or sell?

(v) was the trade an opening or closing transaction?

If you are unsure of any aspects or terms listed on a broker's contract, contact your investment advisor and get clarification.

Opening and Closing Transactions

Two items on the contract have not yet been discussed. One is whether the contract was an opening or closing transaction. An initial trade is an opening transaction. For example, in the contract shown above, the investor bought a put. This was an initial trade. If we assume that the investor, at some point in the future, decides to sell the put, it would be a closing transaction and all rights and obligations granted in the first trade would be cancelled.

Another item on the contract that would appear on opening sales only is the term covered or uncovered. These terms affect margin rules and will be discussed later in the strategy portion of this chapter. You should ensure that both opening / closing and covered / uncovered notations reflect your position. And be sure to discuss all differences or errors with your investment advisor.

More Terminology

One big problem with option investing and subsequently developing strategies is the jargon used by investment advisors and investors alike. It's impossible to get away from this jargon though, and we should learn a few more terms. Here are a few of the terms you need to know:

- writing is the same as an opening sell
- naked is the same as uncovered
- strike price is the same as exercise price
- premium is the same as price of the option

Time Value and Intrinsic Value of Options

The premium of an option is the price as set by the marketplace. This price can be broken into two parts – time value and intrinsic value. The following table illustrates some of the options that could be listed on the well-known stock, ACME Manufacturing.

If you were to purchase an ACME five-month 35 call at a price of

Time value and intrinsic value calculations for options are the same as those for rights and warrants.

c = call p = put	ACME market price: $40 PREMIUMS		
Strike prices	2-month	5-month	8-month
35 C 35 P	5.50 .35	6.50 1.00	8.00 1.50
40 C 40 P	2.50 1.75	3.50 2.00	4.75 2.25
45 C 45 P	.75 5.25	1.25 5.75	1.50 6.00

$6.50, you would be purchasing an option with an intrinsic value of $5. The underlying stock trades at $40; you could buy the call, exercise your right to buy the stock at $35, and then sell the stock at $40, for $5 more than you paid for it. So that call is worth at least $5. But this right to buy the stock at $35 can be exercised at any time until the call's expiry. The stock could continue to go up in value. This five-month period has to be worth something to an investor. To work out the call's time value, you subtract the intrinsic value – $5 in this case – from the call's market price. The remaining premium value ($6.60 - $5) is $1.50 and is called the time premium or time value. Simply defined, it's the value investors place on the right to buy ACME Manufacturing stock at $35 per share for the next five months.

This leads to three new phrases: in-the-money, at-the-money, and out-of-the-money. The previous chart illustrates the application of these terms. If an option has intrinsic value, it's in-the-money by that amount. The $35 calls are in-the-money, as are the $45 puts. If an option has no intrinsic value, it's out-of-the-money. The $45 calls are out-of-the-money, as are the $35 puts. And if the strike price and market price of the underlying are the same, the option is at-the-money. The $40 calls and puts are both at-the-money.

While these terms are often used in discussing strategies, it's not necessary to memorize these descriptions to invest and trade options successfully.

Buying and Selling Options

As we've discussed, there are two types of options – puts and calls – and you can buy or sell either one. Let's look at both the purchase and the sale of an option so you'll see what rights and obligations you would have.

In all the options graphs you'll see in this chapter, the horizontal axis represents the price of the underlying security, while the vertical axis represents the potential profit or loss on the position itself. The graphs do not take into account any time value that the option may have; only its intrinsic value is represented. This first graph illustrates only a

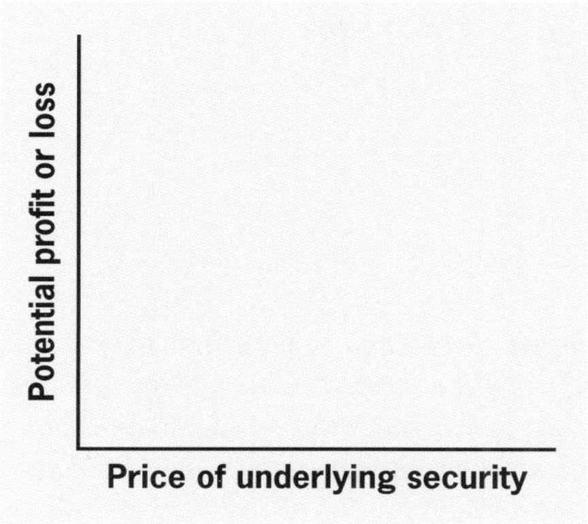

Potential profit or loss

Price of underlying security

call purchase on a stand-alone basis; in other words, assume you hold no other positions in the account.

The Call Buyer

The call buyer pays a premium for the right to buy the underlying security at the strike price any time up until expiration of the option. The call buyer is bullish or is anticipating a rise in the price of the underlying security and will profit if the price of the stock rises. The maximum profit is theoretically unlimited, as it's possible that the stock could rise to infinity. The risk for the call buyer is limited only to the price paid for the call itself; that is, the premium.

The limited risk and unlimited profit characteristics of buying calls make them a popular choice among investors. In this graph, the underlying stock, ABC, trades at $30, while the call has a six month life with a strike price of $30.

The Call Buyer – A Bullish Position

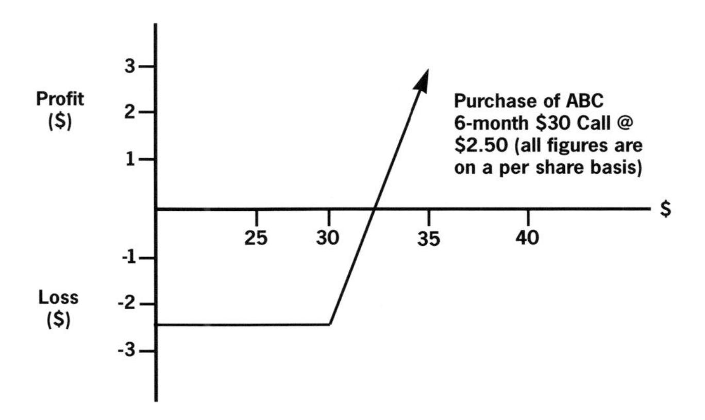

How to read this graph *– The call buyer stands to lose the entire premium paid for the option, (in this case – $2.50) if the market value of ABC is below $30 on expiration of the option. The investor breaks even at $32.50 and will participate dollar for dollar with any stock price movement once ABC rises above $32.50. Profit is unlimited, at least theoretically, as the stock price has no upside limitations.*

The Call Writer

The naked call writer gets a premium to take on the obligation to sell the underlying security at the strike price any time up until expiration of the option. Call writers are neutral to bearish: they want to see the underlying security's price fall in value or at least stay the same. The call writer has a maximum profit potential of the premium, and, like a short seller of stock, has unlimited risk. The stock can theoretically rise in value to infinity, and the writer could be required to purchase the stock at this inflated price, only to have to sell it at the strike price. Risk can be large and profits small.

The naked writer does not own the underlying stock. The covered writer does.

The call writer's position can be illustrated as below, assuming that the call sold is on ABC, has a 90-day life and a strike price of $30. The market price of ABC is $30 and the call trades at $2.50. This is an aggressive strategy for an investor and should be considered only by those investors experienced in short selling.

The Naked Call Writer – A Neutral Position

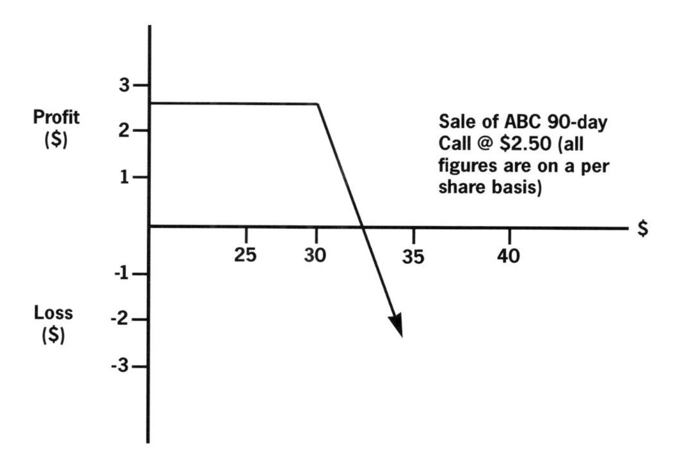

How to read this graph *– The naked call writer profits if the underlying security falls in value or at least stays the same. But profit is limited to the premium. Losses can be theoretically unlimited as the underlying security's price can rise to infinity. The stock can rise in price to $32.50, the break-even price, before the investor loses money. But after that point, the investor would lose dollar for dollar with any price movement in the stock.*

The Put Buyer

A put buyer obtains rights for premiums paid. A put buyer has the right to sell the underlying security at any time until the expiration day at the strike price stipulated in the contract. Put buyers are bearish or negative on the outlook for the underlying security and want to profit from decreasing market values.

The stock, ABC, is currently trading at $30 and the put being considered for purchase has a strike price of $30 and a time to expiration of approximately 90 days. The put's market price is $2. This graph illustrates that the put buyer has a limited risk and a limited reward. The maximum profit to be made on the position is the exercise price of the put after costs and expenses. This is assuming that the stock falls to a price of zero.

The Put Buyer — A Bearish Position

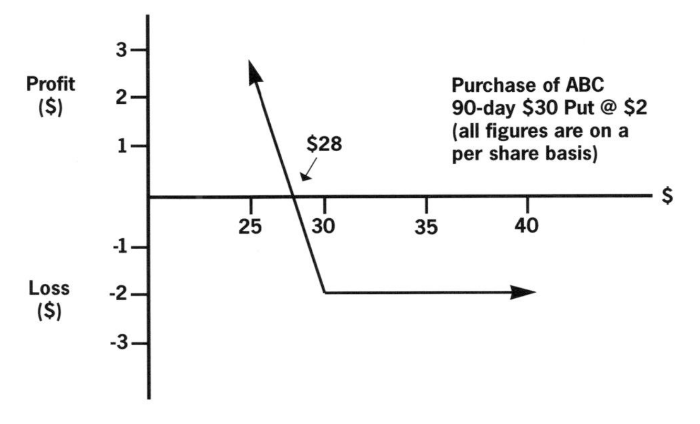

How to read this graph *– If the investor buys a put for $2, all that can be lost is $2, even if the stock rises to $40 or more. If the stock falls in value, the investor will break even (recoup the entire investment) at $28. If the stock continues to fall below $28, the investment will be profitable, doubling at $26. Maximum profit of $28 will occur at 0.*

The Put Writer

The put seller or writer, on the other hand, takes on the obligation to buy the underlying security at the strike price until expiry, and gets a premium for the trouble. This obligation can be enforced at any time up until the option's expiration. Put sellers are usually considered bullish to neutral, as they will profit if the underlying security stays above the strike or exercise price. The maximum profit that the put writer can make is the premium received from the sale of the put, and this maximum profit will be made if the put itself has little or no market value on the expiration day.

To illustrate how this position would compare to that of purchasing stock, let's assume that the stock, ABC, is still trading at $30. This time we are going to write a six-month put with a strike price of $30 and a premium of $3. The maximum profit, illustrated on the graph, occurs if the stock stays above $30: nobody would want to sell us their stock at $30 if it's worth more than that, and of course we would keep the premium of $3. If, however, the stock falls below $30, we would be forced to fulfill the obligation of buying the stock. Our worst case scenario would occur if the stock dropped all the way to zero; we would still be obligated to buy what was now a worthless stock at $30. Our loss would then be $30 less the $3 premium we had received, or $27.

The Put Writer – A Bullish Position

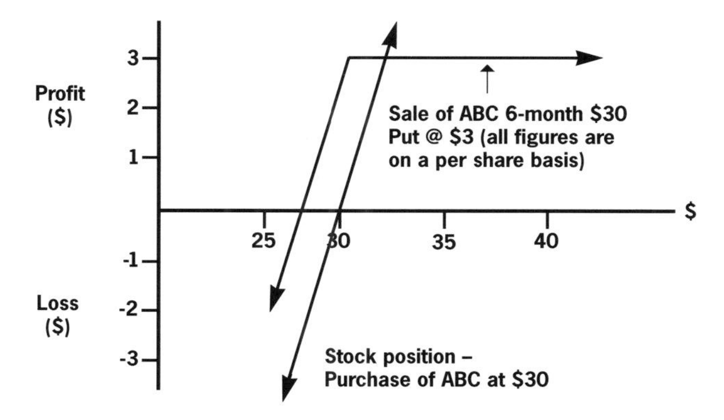

How to read this graph *– If the investor writes a put for $3, all that can be earned or made on the position is the $3 premium, even if the stock rises to $40. Because the $3 premium creates a cushion for the investor, the stock can fall to a price of $27 before there is any loss. If the stock continues to fall*

in value, the investor is at risk. The maximum loss occurs at $0. The investor is obligated to buy a worthless stock for $30. Because of the $3 premium received, the maximum loss is $27 per share.

Call Buying and Put Writing are Not the Same

The Four Basic Positions

- **buying calls**
- **writing naked calls**
- **buying puts**
- **writing naked puts**

These four positions are the building blocks that the options investor can use to construct different investment strategies designed to protect assets, earn income, or participate in the price movement of various securities. If you understand these four positions clearly, with their attendant rights and obligations, designing a specific strategy becomes much easier.

It's often said that call buying and put writing or selling are comparable. While both strategies are bullish, they should not be considered interchangeable. Call buyers have rights, unlimited profit potential and limited risk. Put writers have limited profit potential and limited though substantial risk. Put writers have obligations, not rights. Call buying is an alternative to put selling, but isn't a substitute.

The same comparison exists with put buyers and call writers. The put buyer has rights, limited risk, and limited profit, although it can be substantial. The naked call writer has obligations, limited profit, and unlimited risk. The put buying strategy is an alternative to call writing but isn't a substitute.

A Word of Caution

Put writing is an aggressive strategy that may be quite profitable for an investor during buoyant markets, but should only be attempted if you can pay for the stock position that you might be obligated to buy. It's quite possible to assume too large a financial obligation because the money required to finance the position can be less than the alternative stock position. As well, the dollar amount of the premium can sometimes entice investors into taking on more risk than they can afford. This is one of the dangers of investing in options.

How Time Affects Options

One aspect to options trading that is sometimes misunderstood is the time factor and its influence on the price of an option. Options are wasting assets; they have a limited, preset lifespan and one day, sooner than the investor often realizes, they will expire. Options have a time value, and as the expiry date for the option approaches, the time value decreases. Most investors wrongly assume that the cost of time is linear. So, if a three-month option had a time value of $1, then a six-month option would have a time value of $2. This linear interpretation of time value could be depicted graphically as:

A Linear Time Value Decay

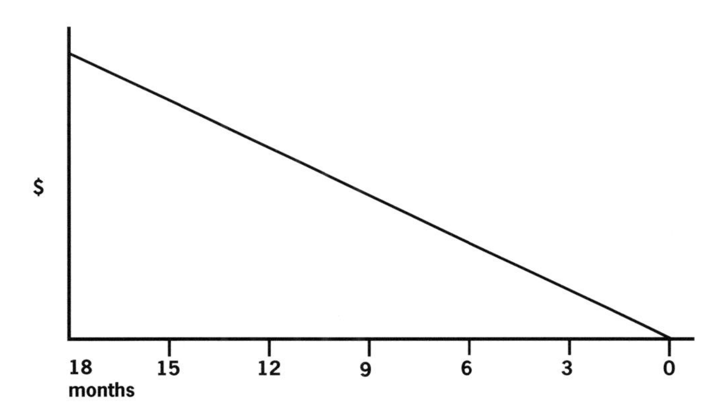

How to read this graph *– The option's time value is highest, all things being equal, at the beginning of the option's life. As time marches on, this value decreases daily by an equal amount. This is a misconception.*

But time value isn't linear. It decays on an accelerated basis in the final months and weeks, which looks more like:

How Time Value Really Decays

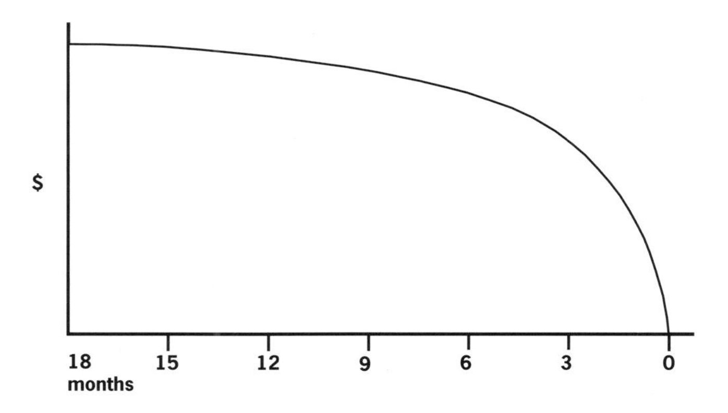

How to read this graph *– As previously illustrated, the option's time value is highest at the beginning of its life. As time until expiry shortens, the time premium attributed to the option begins to decrease, with the most dramatic moves taking place in the final months and weeks before expiration.*

Accordingly, the cost of a six-month option will be more than a four-month option; and the four-month option will be worth more than the two-month option, but not by a proportional amount. The time value of an option decreases little over its lifetime, until about the three or four month mark; then it disappears quickly. It's vital to understand this time value decay, because taking advantage of this aspect of an option's price is essential to successful trading.

In choosing which option to buy or sell, time must be as important a consider-ation as the cost.

Often investors looking at buying an option will choose the cheapest option, basing the investment decision on the actual dollar cost. As you can see from the preceding graph, time value decreases rapidly as expiry approaches. Not only are you fighting the market, hoping that events will occur as forecast, but you are also fighting the clock. So buying the cheapest option with only a few weeks of life left is a fool's game. In choosing which option to buy or sell, time must be as important a consideration as the cost.

Time value, then, affects the price of an option; the longer the time to expiry, the greater the option's value. Other factors that affect option prices are interest rates, dividends on the underlying common shares and, of course, the relationship of the strike price of the option to the stock price. Another key factor is how volatile the underlying stock's market price is. The following chart indicates how each of these factors would affect an option's price if that factor changed in isolation. An understanding of how each of the factors really relates to the option is beyond the scope of this book, but understanding the results of any changes in these factors is important.

Factors Affecting Options Premiums

	Put Premium	Call Premium
Interest Rates Up	↓	↑
Interest Rates Down	↑	↓
Dividend Yield Up	↑	↓
Dividend Yield Down	↓	↑
Volatility Up	↑	↑
Volatility Down	↓	↓

Using Options as Investment Vehicles

To really understand options, it helps to take a closer look at some of the strategies that investors can use to further their objectives. By calculating the investment parameters such as cost, potential return on capital invested and the amount at risk, the characteristics of each strategy, and the market conditions in which it should work, can be clearly outlined. You can make your decision and choose your strategy on an informed basis.

Let's use two separate scenarios to illustrate the use of the four basic option positions. A final illustration on covered writing will complete our review.

Setting the Stage

For all illustrations, the following assumptions apply:

- options are American-style;

- no dividends are payable on the stock;
- commissions are not included;
- income and other taxes are not accounted for;
- your account holds only the position under discussion;
- all returns are calculated over the period discussed and are not annualized.

Scenario One

You are bullish on ACME Co. stock, currently trading at $40. There are three possible strategies that are appropriate in this situation:

- buying the stock itself;
- buying ACME $40 calls; or
- selling ACME $40 puts.

Scenario One – Bullish on ACME

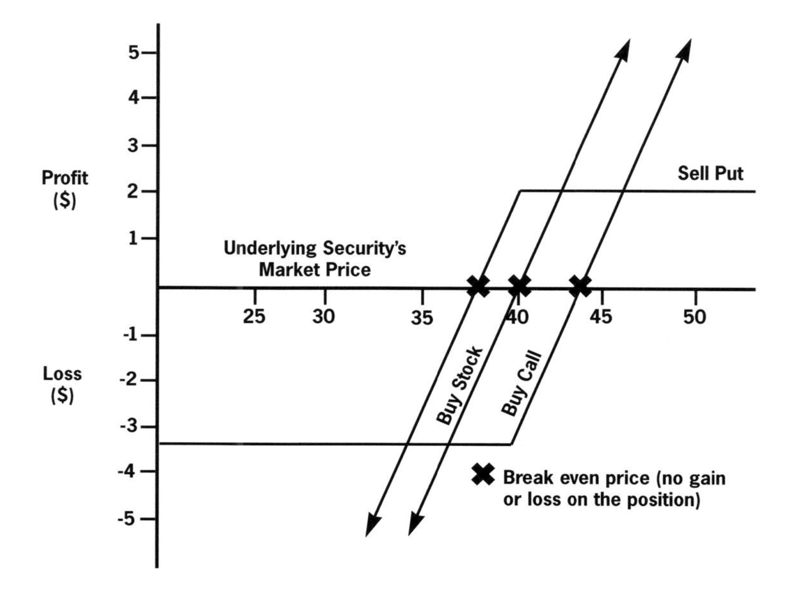

Strategy One – Buy Stock	**Strategy Two – Buy Calls**	**Strategy Three – Sell Puts**
Buy 500 ACME @ $40 Cost = $20,000	Buy 5 ACME 5-month 40 calls @ $3.50 Cost = $1,750	Buy 5 ACME 5-month 40 puts @ $2.00 Premium Received = $1,000 Margin Required = $5,000 (The credit received must stay in the account.)
A. Positive scenario – the stock rises in value by $4.00 over a 4-month time period.		
Sell 500 ACME @ $44	Sell 5 5-month 40 calls @ $6.25	Sell 5 5-month 40 puts @ $0.25
Total Received............$22,000	Total Received..............$3,125	(to close out position)
Less Cost..................$20,000	Less Cost.....................$1,750	Total Paid.........................-$125
Profit............................$2,000	Profit............................$1,375	Plus Premium...............$1,000
		Profit.............................$875
Return...............................10%	Return...............................79%	Return...........................17.5%
B. Negative scenario – stock drops in value by $4.00 over a 4-month time period.		
Sell 500 ACME @ $36	Sell 5 5-month 40 calls @ $0.50	Sell 5 5-month 40 puts @ $4.75
Total Received............$18,000	Total Received.................$250	(to close out position)
Less Cost..................$20,000	Less Cost..................- $1,750	Total Paid.......................$2,375
Profit............................$2,000	Loss............................$1,500	Plus Premium...............$1,000
		Loss.............................$1,375
Return..............................-10%	Return............................- 86%	Return..........................-27.5%
C Typical scenario – nothing happens and the stock remains at $40. Time simply runs out on the options.		
Sell 500 ACME @ $40	Sell 5 5-month 40 calls @ $1.00	Sell 5 5-month 40 puts @ $0.75
Total Received............$20,000	Total Received.................$500	(to close out position)
Less Cost..................$20,000	Less Cost...................$1,750	Total Paid.........................$375
Balance.................................0	Loss............................$1,250	Plus Premium...............$1,000
		Profit..............................$675
Return.................................0%	Return..........................- 71.4%	Return..........................-27.5%
Returns for Strategly Three are based on the deposit margin required, i.e. $5,000.		
	Summary	
D. Dollar risk in the position: Total Cost or $20,000 Per share = $40.00	Total Cost or $17,500 Per share = $3.50	Difference between the strike price and premium received ($20,000 less $1,000) or $19,000 Per share = $38,000
The total risk in all the positions occurs if the stock does not rise as expected and instead drops in price.		
E. Maximum loss occurs at: Zero – the stock cannot be sold and all capital is lost.	Below $40.00 – the call expires worthless.	Zero – the put is exercised and you must purchase the stock at $40.00. Your cost is $40 less the $2 premium, or $38.00.
F Maximum Potential Reward: Unlimited – the stock could rise to infinity.	Unlimited – the stock could rise to a price of infinity (but unlike the stock, the option eventually expires.)	Limit – $1,000: the premium received.

Strategy #1 – Buying Stock

There are some key differences between these three strategies. The first strategy – buying stock – is a long-term proposition. You can earn dividend income, if available, and participate in any rise in the security's price. Likewise, a drop in the security will create a loss, and the potential risk could equal the stock's total purchase price, or $20,000, if ACME dropped to zero.

Strategy #2 – Buying Calls

In contrast, the second strategy – which involves a long call position – offers a great deal of leverage. There is a much lower dollar risk ($1,750 vs. $20,000), but the likelihood of losing all your money is greater. The call offers unlimited profit potential, but only for five months, and before you can participate dollar for dollar with ACME's price movement, the initial investment of $1,750 must be recouped. This occurs at $43.50. Of course, the leverage is that two-edge sword we spoke about earlier. The call's upside potential is attractive even with a small move in ACME's price. In this example, a 10% move on the stock price equates to a return of 79% – not a bad return. Often novice investors will decide that with such attractive returns, they should invest an equal dollar amount, so that here, you would purchase closer to 55 contracts than five. If you normally buy 500 shares of stock, you are wiser to purchase five contracts, covering 500 shares. You should not overextend the leverage on the position, which could prove a fatal mistake.

Strategy #3 – Writing Puts

The third strategy – writing puts – is quite a bit different from the other two, but does fit the overall parameter. It's bullish. This strategy performs even when the other strategies do not – when the stock's market price is flat. It's a short position – something similar to shorting stock – and carries with it a risk unlike that of the call strategy. There is a margin requirement to establish the position. The put writer must be willing to purchase the stock at the strike price if required to do so. In other words, the put writer must buy the stock at the $40 strike price even if it has fallen to zero. That's the risk in this strategy. When the writer least wants to buy the stock – there it is. Of course a writer can purchase the put at any time in the secondary market before it's exercised and close out the position. Once the put has been assigned or exercised, though, this recourse isn't available.

If, in fact, the put writer was required to buy the stock because the holder exercised the put, there are still alternatives available. If the stock is thought of as a buy – the outlook still remains bullish or positive – the investor should simply hold the stock for a price recovery. If further weakness looks possible, the stock should be sold and the loss taken before the price of the stock drops further. If the outlook were neutral to bullish, the strategy that is best employed is the covered write – a hedging strategy popular with income-oriented investors that will be illustrated later on.

To sum up:

(i) The long stock position offers the investor income potential if dividends are paid, capital gains potential and returns commensurate with the price movement of the stock. Time isn't a factor because, barring any unforeseen events, the stock has no expiry.

(ii) The long call position offers leverage. For a portion of the cost of the long stock position, you can almost replicate the upside potential of the stock and at the same time severely limit the dollar risk. But, and it's a big but, time to expiry is a limiting factor.

(iii) The short put position offers income earning potential in neutral to bullish markets, and is levered, as the margin is less than the cost of the stock. Time is on your side, as the faster it runs out, the quicker the profit is booked. But risk is higher in this position so you have to monitor events carefully.

Scenario Two

In this example, you are bearish on ACME Co., still trading at $40 per share. You have three choices for an investment strategy:

- sell the stock short;
- buy a put on ACME; or
- write an ACME call.

Scenario Two – Bearish on ACME

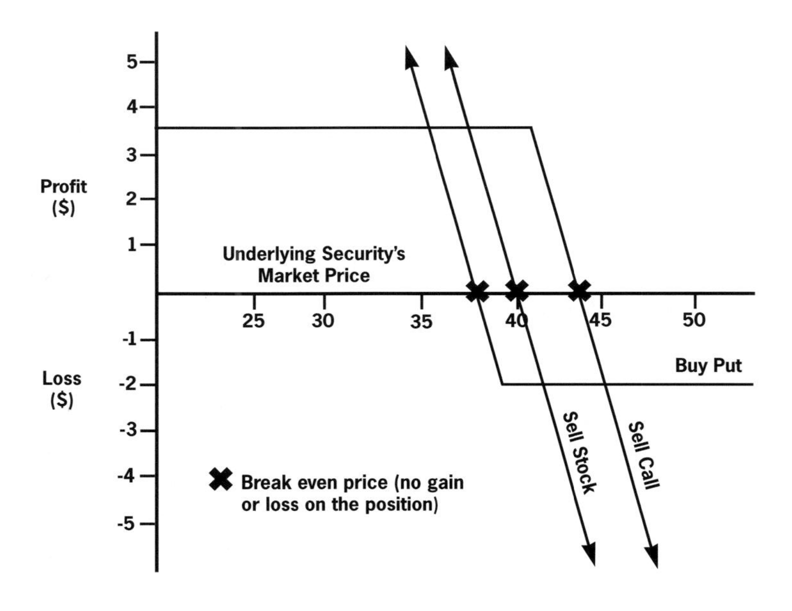

Strategy One – Sell Stock Short	Strategy Two – Buy Puts	Strategy Three – Sell Calls
Buy 500 ACME @ $40 Credit Received = $20,000 Margin Required = $6,000 (The credit received must stay in the account.)	Buy 5 ACME 5-month 40 calls @ $2.00 Cost = $1,000	Buy 5 ACME 5-month 40 puts @ $3.50 Credit Received = $1,750 Margin Required = $5,000 (The credit received must stay in the account.)
A. Positive scenario – the stock falls in value by $4.00 over a 4-month time period.		
Buy 500 ACME @ $36 Total Cost....................$18,000 Less Sale Proceeds....$20,000 Profit............................$2,000 Return..............................33%	Sell 5 ACME 5-month 40 puts @ $4.00 Total Received..............$2,000 Less Cost....................$1,000 Profit............................$1,000 Return............................100%	Buy 5 ACME 5-month 40 calls @ $0.75 Total Received..............$1,750 Less Cost........................$375 Profit............................$1,375 Return............................27.5%
B. Negative scenario – the stock rises in value by $4.00 over a 4-month time period.		
Buy 500 ACME @ $44 Total Cost....................$22,000 Less Proceeds...........$20,000 Loss............................$2,000 Return.............................- 10%	Sell 5 ACME 5-month 40 puts @ $0.25 Total Proceeds.................$125 Less Cost..................- $1,000 Loss............................- $875 Return..........................- 87.5%	Buy 5 ACME 5-month 40 calls @ $4.75 Total Received..............$1,750 (from original sale) Less Cost....................$2,375 Loss.............................- $625 Return..........................- 12.5%
C Typical scenario – nothing happens and the stock remains at $40. Time simply runs out.		
Buy 500 ACME @ $40 Total Received............$20,000 Less Cost..................$20,000 Balance.................................0 Return................................0%	Sell 5 5-month ACME 40 puts @ $0.25 Total Received.................$125 Less Cost....................$1,000 Profit...............................$875 Return...........................-87.5%	Buy 5 5-month 40 calls @ $0.50 Total Received..............$1,750 Less Cost........................$250 Profit................ ....$1,500 Return...............................30%
Returns for Strategly One and Three are based on the deposit margin required.		
	Summary	
D. Dollar risk in the position: Unlimited	Total Cost or $1,000	Unlimited
The total risk in all the positions occurs if the stock does not fall as expected and instead rises in price.		
E. Maximum loss occurs at: Infinity – theoretically the stock can rise to infinity.	$40.00 and above – the put expires worthless.	Infinity – theoretically the underlying stock can rise to infinity.
F. Maximum Potential Reward: $40 per share or $20,000 – or the total value of the stock if it's market price falls to zero.	$40.00 per share less the cost of the put if the market price of the stock falls to zero by expiry.	$3.50 per share if the price of the stock falls below $40 by expiry.

Strategy #1 – Selling Stock Short

Scenario Two also has some key differences between its three strategies. Selling stock short is an aggressive strategy that should only be attempted by those investors willing and able to accept the risks involved. Maintaining the short position for extended periods of time is expensive in terms of interest lost on capital, and dividends, which must be paid by the short seller. It could be years before the market realizes that a particular stock is overvalued.

Strategy #2 – Buying Puts

The put strategy offers the investor a limited risk position with much the same characteristics as the short stock position. While participation in terms of falling stock prices is initially curtailed because of the cost of the put, which must first be recouped, its risk limitations and non-responsibility for dividends make buying a put an attractive alternative to short selling.

Strategy #3 – Selling Calls

The short call, on the other hand, is similar to the short stock position, as risk is unlimited. There is a cushion of $3.50 per share, the premium of the call. If the stock begins to rise, you won't lose capital until the stock rises above $43.50. Another risk, of course, is the payment of a dividend on the stock. It's possible that a call writer may be exercised for the dividend payment. This is a risk that should be discussed at length with your investment advisor. One advantage writing a call does have over the short sale of the stock itself is that the stock can remain static and the short call position will still be profitable.

To sum up:

(i) The short stock position offers the investor capital gains potential commensurate with the market price of the security. Time isn't a factor, but risks are substantial. Dividends and margin calls are also risks that cannot be fully known in advance.

(ii) Buying a put offers the investor leverage. For a portion of the margin required for the short position, you can almost replicate the profit potential of the short stock position and at the same time limit the dollar risk to the premium only. Time is a limiting factor.

(iii) The short call position more closely replicates the short stock position, in that risk on the upside is in lockstep with the short stock position once the break-even price has been reached. But profit is limited. This is a position in which time is working for you. This strategy is suitable for downward movements in the underlying stock's price. Risk is high and the position should be monitored closely.

Covered Writing

Another strategy that doesn't really fit with the previous examples is covered call writing. This conservative strategy takes advantage of the same accelerated decay in time premiums that can so work against an option buyer. While gains are possible, the potential isn't as great as buying and trading options positions. However, you can maintain an attractive level of return even in bear markets.

The covered write involves:

(i) buying (or holding) the underlying security

(ii) writing a call against this position

So, on one hand, you own the stock, and, on the other, you have the potential obligation to deliver it at the strike price. Covered writing allows you to maintain an investment and get any income derived from it while taking advantage of the options market.

Covered call writing is a balancing act that can smooth out returns over the long run. The investor who writes consistently against the portfolio may not experience the peak of the market in terms of return; but also should not suffer the full extent of the lows. There is a premium cushion that softens the effect of tumbling market prices.

Covered call writing is a balancing act that can smooth out returns over the long run.

For example, say you own 500 shares of ACME at a $40 cost price. You want to continue holding the stock, but you would like to earn some money now and decide to sell or write a call, using the five month 40 calls @ $3.50.

The following graph illustrates your position:

The Covered Write – A Neutral Position on ACME

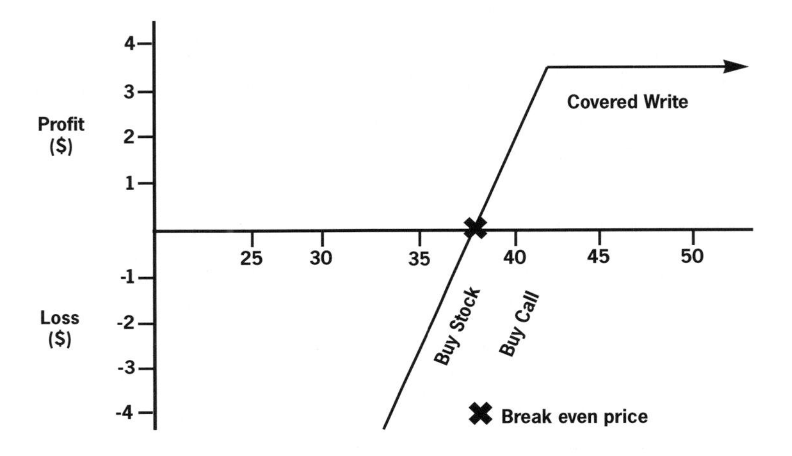

The first thing you should recognize is that the risk in the position is really in the stock. Since you own the stock, the risk of losing money depends on what happens to its market price. The total risk is equal to the cost of the stock. This dollar risk is reduced by the premium received from the sale of the call, in this case $3.50 per share. So risk is $40 (the stock's cost) less $3.50, or $36.50 per share. The total dollar risk is equal to $36.50 x 500 or $18,250. The potential profit on this position is limited, as the call could obligate you to sell the underlying position any time until expiration. For this obligation you would get $3.50 per share or $1,750 for 500 shares. The return can be calculated as

$$\frac{\$1{,}750}{18{,}250} = 9.6\%$$

If the stock were to fall in price, you would not have to worry about losing any money until it reached $36.50. Below that price you would participate in further price declines in the stock. If the stock rises above the strike price of $40, you would not participate at all, unless you bought the call back and closed the trade out.

Covered writing is a popular strategy for conservative investors because of the flexibility it offers in controlling risk. By choosing a strike price above the underlying security's market price, you can be more aggressive. And by lowering the strike price, the strategy becomes more conservative.

As you probably have concluded by now, there's much to learn about options. Yet, we've we've barely touched the surface! So far, we've only talked about listed equity options, but there are many more strategies and products to consider when investing in options. One way to begin to really understand the product is to chart both several listed options and their underlying securities. This will help you get a better understanding of how options move in relation to the stock.

Getting Started in Options

While more and more investors are taking direct control of their investments these days, options are one area where it pays to proceed cautiously and seek out expert advice. Choosing an investment advisor who is registered to trade options, knowledgeable, and helpful is a good start. Here are some other tips that will help make investing in options a pleasant and rewarding experience.

Options is one area where it pays to proceed cautiously and seek out expert advice.

Guidelines for Buying Options

- Make sure you thoroughly understand what is involved before you enter an order.
- Buy enough time for the idea to work. Don't be caught short on time.
- Set a price for the option that you are willing to pay in terms of risk. Don't chase an option.

- Clarify goals and objectives before the trade is initiated. Set your breakeven price in advance in case the market goes against you.
- Consider carefully the risk or leverage you are assuming – don't buy more than you can afford to lose.
- Be objective and flexible – consider all alternatives.
- Diversify into different underlying securities.
- Maintain a disciplined approach to trading.

Guidelines for Covered Writing

If you are thinking about a covered writing strategy, here's a few more things to think about:

- Choose the stock, not the return.
- Write options with three to six months left until expiry.
- Be flexible – adjust the strategy if the stock price moves sharply.
- If the outlook on the stock changes to negative – close out both the stock and option position, as your short call will not compensate for a loss in share value.
- You may be forced to sell the stock – are you prepared for that?

A Final Word

Other products that may look and act like options are convertible preferreds and convertible debentures. If you strip away the preferred or debenture part of the security, what remains is the conversion privilege, which is like a call option. And the astute investor will use the options market to price such conversion features.

In this chapter, we've simply described the more commonplace option products – those based on equities. Other products include options on bonds, currencies, indexes, commodity futures, and silver and gold too. You can also find option-like characteristics embedded in other investment vehicles, such as convertible preferreds and debentures. And while you may never trade a listed option, the likelihood of trading a vehicle with an embedded option is high. Hopefully, this chapter will help you understand and invest in these products with a greater sense of confidence.

Summary

Options are derivative products – they are derived from another security, often a stock. They allow you to buy or sell a stock or other type of security at a fixed price for a fixed period. They usually trade for more than their intrinsic value, as investors are willing to pay for the leverage potential they offer over a period. In these respects they resemble rights and warrants, but there are some differences too. Options are issued by a third party rather than by the company that issued the underlying stock, and they trade on an options market rather than a stock market, although the options market may be situated on the stock market floor.

The option issuer is called the writer, the price of the option is its premium, and the price at which the stock can be bought or sold is the strike price. There are two types of options: calls and puts. A call gives you the right to buy shares at a certain price for a certain period, whereas a put lets you sell them. A call writer takes on the obligation to sell these shares if asked to do so, and a put writer must buy them if required. The option holder decides whether to exercise the option, sell it, or let it expire, and the option writer acts according to the holder's decision.

There are four basic options positions that an investor can undertake: buy a call, write a call, buy a put and write a put. Each reflects a certain outlook on the underlying stock, each can be used to accomplish certain goals, and each has its own degree of risk and reward. Call writers who own the underlying security are known as covered writers, and their outlook, goals and risk-reward ratio differ from those of the naked call writer, who does not own the underlying stock. If the call is exercised, the naked writer would have to buy the underlying stock at its current price to sell it to the call holder.

Mutual Funds and other Managed Products.

The merits of hiring an investment professional.

In this chapter, we look at how you can get someone else to make your investment decisions. Many people assume that going this route means you don't need to learn about the markets and only need to be concerned about your portfolio at tax time. It doesn't work like that. You still have to choose who you are going to entrust your money to and you still have to monitor their progress. In many cases, you have to choose the asset class you want to invest in, and you always have to choose which method of professional management you want to go with. We'll look at mutual funds and then at other money management plans.

Mutual Funds: A Great Place to Start

Probably no other investment has received as much publicity as mutual funds. Even so, mutual funds are often misunderstood. And, if you want to avoid pitfalls later on, you should be aware of how mutual funds differ from each other before handing over your life savings.

The mutual fund industry holds about $400 billion of Canadians savings.

Mutual funds are often the investment of choice for first-time investors. Canada's mutual fund industry has ballooned in the past decade, largely because of a flood of new investors seeking a higher rate of return than that available from bank savings accounts and GICs. What began in 1990 as a $30 billion industry now holds about $400 billion of Canadians' savings. And this trend is expected to continue well into the new century.

The Many Benefits of Mutual Funds

Why are mutual funds so popular? For one thing, they come in a variety of sizes and shapes. Through mutual funds, you can hold stocks or bonds, or a blend of the two as well as other investments such as real estate or money market securities. With a single investment, a mutual fund can offer a variety of securities in several different industries – a particular advantage for the small investor with insufficient resources to create a diversified portfolio. And mutual funds are professionally managed, so the mix of investments is regularly readjusted to suit current conditions.

A Few Drawbacks

This doesn't mean, however, that mutual funds are for everybody. Most funds emphasize long-term investment and so are unsuitable if you are seeking spectacular short-term performance. You can double your money on a speculative penny stock in a few months if you pick the right one, but no mutual fund, with its diversified portfolio, can offer that type of return.

Funds that levy sales charges may also deduct these from the initial investment, which also makes purchasing a fund unattractive for the short-term. And even professional money managers can call the market wrong, resulting in a loss for the fund's investors. In fact, most managers of stock mutual funds cannot beat the performance of relevant stock market indexes.

Professional money managers, of course, get paid to manage the money in your fund. This creates an ongoing cost that can significantly cut into your returns.

What is a Mutual Fund?

Investing in a mutual fund means buying shares, or units, in the fund's assets, represented by its portfolio of securities. Mutual funds also are known as open-ended investment funds, because they continuously offer more shares for sale to the public. At the same time, you have the continuing right to withdraw your investment simply by submitting your shares back to the fund and getting the current value per unit. This characteristic is known as the right of redemption, and it's the hallmark of mutual funds.

The price of each mutual fund unit doesn't depend on how many people are buying, but on the market value of the fund's portfolio. And here's where mutual funds differ from other securities. In the case of a mutual fund share, the price equals the fund's NAVPS, or net asset value per share. In other words, if the fund were to liquidate all its securities at their current market value and pay off all its liabilities, the proceeds attributed equally among all the shares would be the net asset value per share. So even though a fund may issue more shares, that won't change the share price because the fund's assets have grown by the same proportion.

$$\textbf{NAVPS} = \frac{\textbf{Assets (including investments - Liabilities)}}{\textbf{Number of shares outstanding}}$$

Although there's no typical price for a mutual fund share, you should be aware that you may be required to pay a sales charge, or commit to paying a redemption fee when you eventually sell the shares. We'll discuss this in more detail later.

Choosing the right mutual fund depends on your investment goals and your ability to tolerate risk. Some investors become comfortable taking increasingly greater risks as their level of sophistication grows over time. With dozens of mutual fund companies offering shares in hundreds of different funds, there is a wide range of choice from the safest money market investments to the riskiest overseas funds.

Mutual Funds are Not Guaranteed

Mutual funds do not have any form of government backing similar to deposit insurance on bank accounts. As with buying stocks or bonds or other securities, the risk of price fluctuations you assume in buying mutual fund shares is all yours to bear. That's why it's important to choose the right fund to match your objectives and risk tolerance.

Mutual fund custodian: a chartered bank or trust company which holds the assets of a mutual fund.

On the other hand, the fund's assets are held by a custodian, not the fund company, so there's no danger of the manager absconding with your money or using it for questionable purposes. As well, the fund's assets are segregated from those of the custodian, and are protected by trust and banking laws.

Another way you can protect yourself is by taking your business to an investment firm that is covered by the Canadian Investor Protection Fund (CIPF). This industry-supported fund protects clients from firms in the unlikely event they become insolvent. It doesn't protect you from poor performance on your funds. The coverage is capped at $1,000,000 per account.

Make Sure You Read the Prospectus

To learn about a fund's investment goals, you should begin by reading the offering prospectus, which will describe the degree of safety or risk involved, whether the fund's prime objective is income or capital gain, and the main types of securities in its investment portfolio. A fund prospectus can either be obtained by contacting an investment advisor or by calling the mutual fund company directly. Prospectuses can also be viewed and downloaded off the Web by going to www.sedar.com. Business sections of most of the major daily newspapers publish monthly mutual fund surveys.

Mutual Funds Can Meet Most Investors' Objectives

Many companies that offer a variety of mutual funds let you transfer between funds without any extra charge. This gives you a convenient way to readjust your own portfolio of funds as market conditions and personal circumstances change. Based on their differing investment objectives, there are a few main types of funds from which to choose.

Money Market Funds

These funds became popular with investors during the 1980s and 1990s, and still represent one of the largest categories of mutual funds. They aim to achieve a high level of income and liquidity by investing in short-term money market instruments such as treasury bills, commercial paper and short-term government bonds. These funds are a good place to park your money while pondering longer term investments, however, they offer limited opportunity for capital gain. This is reflected by the fact that money market funds keep the net asset value at a set level, typically $10, by distributing monthly income to unit holders in cash or new units.

Income or Bond Funds

These funds emphasize safety of principal and high income. They invest mainly in good quality, high yielding government and corporate debt securities, some high-yield preferred and common shares and mortgages. Unit prices of income funds hold quite steady when interest rates are stable, but they can move sharply during periods of interest rate volatility.

Mortgage Funds

Mortgage funds have investment goals similar to bond funds, and unit values are affected by similar economic factors. Fund investors hold a share in a group of mortgages, much as bond fund investors hold a share in a group of bonds, rather than holding title to a particular property.

Balanced Funds

Balanced funds have as their main investment objective a mixture of safety, income and capital appreciation. To achieve this, the funds hold a balanced portfolio of fixed-income securities for stability and income, plus a broad group of common stock holdings for diversification, dividend income and growth potential. The balance between defensive and aggressive security holdings is rarely 50-50. Rather, balanced fund managers adjust the percentage of each part of the total portfolio to reflect current market conditions and future expectations.

Common Stock or Equity funds

These funds invest chiefly in common shares. They may buy short-term notes or other fixed income securities in limited amounts for diversification, income and liquidity. However, the bulk of the assets are in common shares in the pursuit of capital gain. Since common share prices are typically more volatile than other investment types, net asset values of equity funds tend to fluctuate more widely. Some equity funds invest in a variety of overseas markets as well as Canada and the United States, looking globally for the greatest opportunity for growth. As with common stocks, equity funds range greatly in degree of risk and growth potential. Some are broadly diversified, heavily invested in blue-chip, income-yielding common shares and may, therefore, be classified at the conservative end of the equity fund scale. Others adopt a more aggressive investment approach, seeking capital gains at the sacrifice of some safety and income.

Specialty Funds

Specialty funds are those that concentrate their holdings on shares of a group of companies in one industry, in one geographic location or in one segment of the capital market. While still offering some diversification in their portfolios, they are more vulnerable to swings in the industry in which they specialize. If the portfolio contains foreign securities, there also could be the risk of changes in currency values. Many specialty funds, but not all, tend to be more speculative than most types of common share funds.

Global Funds

These funds seek gains and diversification by investing in markets that offer the best prospects, regardless of location. Some global funds are invested in bonds, others are equity funds and still others are money market funds.

Dividend Funds

Dividend funds invest mostly in high quality preferred and sometimes common shares of taxable Canadian corporations to get maximum dividend income. Most also hold a small proportion of bonds for their fixed interest payments.

Real Estate Funds

These funds invest in income-producing property such as shopping centres to achieve long-term growth through capital appreciation and the reinvestment of income.

Ethical Funds

Ethical funds make investment decisions based on moral criteria, which vary from fund to fund. One ethical fund may avoid investing in companies that profit from tobacco, alcohol or armaments, while another fund may invest according to religious beliefs.

Index Funds

So far, we've talked about *active* fund managers. These managers decide what particular securities to buy and sell, and when. They try to beat the overall stock or bond market.

But there's another way to invest, called indexing. And you can do it with mutual funds. You can buy a stock index fund or a bond index fund. Index funds merely try to match the returns of the targeted index by holding a basket of component stocks or bonds. Some use derivatives to mimic the returns of the index.

Not having a portfolio manager translates into lower ongoing costs.

The TSE also has a Total Return Index, which does include reinvested dividends and could therefore be fairly compared to the return on an equity mutual fund.

Clone Funds

So-called "clone" funds have been created to skirt foreign content rules for RRSPs and other registered plans. These rules limit foreign content in your RRSP to a certain percentage of the total cost of your plan's investments. Clone funds closely track the returns of actively managed foreign stock funds while still counting as 100% Canadian content.

Clone funds are classed as Canadian content because most of their money is invested in safe, short-term Canadian investments. The funds get exposure to the foreign mutual funds they aim to track through complex investments called over-the-counter derivatives. When the foreign mutual fund's value increases, the clone fund earns an almost identical increase in value on the derivatives. When the foreign fund's value declines, the loss on the derivatives causes the clone fund's value to drop in near lockstep with the foreign fund.

The derivatives may be forward contracts with a Canadian bank.

Clone funds have higher Management Expense Ratios (MERs) than the active fund that they copy, reflecting the cost of the special cloning feature. There's the additional expense of the forward contracts, plus added operational expenses. These extra annual costs would likely be between 0.50% and 1.5% more than the foreign funds they copy. This means many of these funds have Management Expense Ratio (MERs) of more than 3% and even up to 4.5%.

Your return from clone funds are taxed the same as interest income, at your full tax rate.

Your returns from clone funds are taxed the same as interest income, at your full tax rate. This is the case even though the returns may be mainly or partly from capital gains. Earnings from regular actively managed funds generally are taxed at a lower rate since these earnings would typically be counted as capital gains. So if you're considering using these funds, they should be held inside a tax-deferred plan such as your RRSP. You might consider using clone funds if you've already maximized your RRSP's foreign content and want to add more.

Clones were introduced in 1999 when the foreign content limit for RRSPs was 18% of the book value of your RRSP. With the foreign content limit boosted to 25% in 2000 and to 30% in 2001, the popularity of clones will likely diminish.

How to Evaluate a Mutual Fund

With so many different funds around, how do you select a suitable one? There is no simple answer because, even after putting aside the specialty funds, there are hundreds of funds offering just plain vanilla Canadian stocks and bonds.

Getting advice from an investment advisor could help steer you through the mutual fund maze. Even so, if you possess the skills to judge a mutual fund on your own, then you'll be better equipped to ask the right questions, and get the right answers.

The mutual fund surveys published monthly in the business sections of many major newspapers are a good place to start your research. These provide valuable information on how a fund measures up against its peers. There is information on a fund's various fees, collectively known as the management expense ratio (MER), and on sales commissions, or loads. The tables show whether a fund is eligible for inclusion in a Registered Retirement Savings Plan. There is also data on each fund's historical rate of return over various periods. Typically, these show how the fund fared over the past one month, six months, one year, three years, five years and ten years.

Looking at a fund's past performance gives some idea of how well a fund manager has coped with changing market conditions.

As you know, history is no sure guide to the future. A fund with a bright past could falter next week, especially if market conditions suddenly change. Conversely, a weak performing fund might prompt its management to change their investment approach, and the fund could emerge a winner. Still, looking at a fund's past performance, especially over an extended period, gives some idea of how well a fund manager has coped with changing market conditions in the past.

The Importance of Comparing Similar Funds

When comparing performance records, it's important not to compare two funds that have different investment objectives, such as an equity and a fixed income fund. Behind a higher rate of return in an equity fund, there's also a higher degree of risk. Comparisons with stock exchange indices, such as the TSE 300 Composite Index, also can be misleading. Unlike mutual funds, some stock market indices don't include the added returns from reinvesting dividends.

Buying Mutual Funds

There are three main ways that mutual fund companies market their shares to the public. Most companies sell their products through investment dealers and mutual fund sales companies. A few companies, including all the chartered banks, market their mutual funds directly to the public. The third marketing route is for a fund company to have commissioned sales representatives. The main distinction between these methods is that dealers and commissioned sales representatives advise clients on which mutual funds best suit their personal investment goals and, in the case of a dealer, can offer funds from a variety of fund companies. Direct marketers are more likely to sell funds without a sales charge; however, they sell their own funds only.

Unlike stocks, which are generally bought in board lots of 100, mutual fund investments can be made without regard to how many shares are being bought. Instead, you decide how much money you want to invest. The fund company then issues the corresponding number of shares, even if this involves fractions of shares. The only restriction is that fund companies normally set a minimum dollar amount that they will accept from you as an initial lump-sum purchase. Some mutual funds have initial minimum purchase levels in the $200 to $500 range, but most require a minimum of $1,000. There are also minimum dollar amounts for subsequent cash purchases, perhaps in the $20 to $100 range.

Accumulation Purchase Plans

Most mutual fund companies also have so-called accumulation purchase plans. These let you acquire more shares in the fund periodically. They might require a lower minimum initial investment than lump-sum purchases.

Accumulation plans appeal to people who cannot make large cash investments all at once. They also appeal to individuals interested in dollar-cost averaging. You can also add to your mutual fund holdings by reinvesting dividends the fund pays you. Many funds do this automatically unless you tell them otherwise.

Take a Close Look at Fees

It's well worth investigating sales charges and other fees before buying a mutual fund. Direct marketers generally don't provide much investment advice, but, at the same time, the funds they sell usually don't carry a sales charge. They are known in the industry as no-load funds. Most no-load funds are sold by the big banks, which market their products through their branch networks, and through some independent companies. For investors who know just what they want, or for purchases of straightforward products, such as money market funds, a no-load company might offer the best value.

But not everyone wants to make major investment decisions without the benefit of professional advice. After all, these decisions could affect your net worth. That's where dealers and commissioned sales representatives come in. A few percentage points in sales commissions today might be a small price to pay for making the most appropriate investment decisions.

Sales Charges Vary

There is no standard when it comes to mutual fund sales charges. Instead, they depend on the type of fund you are buying, how you are buying it, and how much money you are investing. Most often, you'll encounter one of four sales fee structures: no-load, front-end load, back-end load and front- and back-end load.

No-load funds, most often sold by banks, trust companies and some direct sellers, do not charge sales commissions directly. You'll still pay a fee to your advisor called a trailer fee, but it's taken from the fund directly and not charged to you separately. All funds pay trailer fees to advisors, brokerage firms and mutual fund sales companies as long as you keep your money in the fund. Trailer fees, often called service fees, are meant to compensate the selling party for ongoing advice and service given to you on the fund company's behalf. Still, with a no-load fund there's no direct sales fee.

With a front-end load fund, however, you pay a sales charge at the time of purchase. The charge is most often in the range of 2% to 5% of the amount you are investing. What percentage you pay depends on how much you are investing and your relationship with your advisor. Some discount brokerage firms that expect clients to make their own investment decisions waive front-end loads, essentially making them no-load funds. They can do this because they don't have to pay for expensive research or employ investment advisors to help you make your choice. Don't be put off a fund by a high sales charge because a particular fund might be worth it. On the other hand, if two funds are almost identical in every other respect, it makes sense to choose a no-load fund because it puts more of your money to work right away.

The last few years have brought a sharp change in the way Canadians pay for buying mutual funds. Today, the most popular way is to commit to paying a redemption fee when the fund shares are eventually sold. This type of charge, known as a back-end load or a deferred sales charge (DSC), seems to appeal to people's natural tendency to want to buy now and pay later. Often these deferred charges diminish gradually over time, usually six years, until they disappear altogether. The commission, which cannot be negotiated, is highest in the first year – typically 6%. It's important to be committed to holding a fund for six or more years before choosing this option. This will spare you the possible dilemma of selling a fund you no longer want, but hesitating because of the high penalty for cashing out early. If you do, the redemption charge may be levied on the amount of your initial investment or the amount the investment has fallen or grown to. Finding out which is something you'll want to do prior to making your investment.

Many fund companies today give you a choice between a front-end and a back-end load. The so-called optional load fund, lets you go either way. But choosing between a front-end-load, back-end-load or no-load mutual fund isn't as simple as it seems. Although it might be tempting to postpone a sales charge to a later year, or even to pay no sales charge at all, these types of funds have other ways of recouping their costs of distribution. Annual fees, which are deducted from the money in the fund, can be higher in deferred-load and no-load funds than in funds that levy a sales charge up front.

To complicate the picture further, some banks and discount brokers have recently begun to rebate part of the trailer fees they get on back-end load funds and no-load funds to their clients. The practice, which is part of an overall trend toward greater transparency in mutual fund pricing, is intended to recognize the fact that do-it yourself investors require less in the way of service and ongoing investment advice.

Annual Management Expenses Add Up

Once you own shares in a mutual fund, the most prominent fee you encounter is the management fee, which mainly goes toward compensating the fund manager for services. Equity funds generally have higher management fees than bond funds because they require more time and market research to administer. Fees vary widely, although the typical Canadian equity fund has a management fee of about 2% of the fund's assets. On top of this, mutual fund companies normally tack on another fee of 0.25% to 0.50% to cover other services, such as distribution and marketing costs. Added together, these fees are known as the management expense ratio (MER), details of which are contained in the fund's prospectus.

Not included in the MER calculation are the fund's brokerage costs and taxes. Each time a fund makes a trade, it must pay commission in one way or another to a brokerage firm. A fund manager who buys and sells investments often incurs higher brokerage costs than a manager who turns over the portfolio less often. While both funds may report the same MER, the high turnover fund will be more costly to run. High turnover funds often rack up brokerage costs of up to 1% of their assets. Added on top of the MER, these extra expenses can result in the fund earning lower average returns over the long term.

What do these fees mean to you? They could mean a lot. Before you get anything back from your mutual fund investment, the fund company deducts as much as 3.5% of the fund's total assets each year in the example given here. This might not seem like much when markets are rapidly rising. But in a year when markets are flat or down, management still takes its fees.

You can compare the historic returns and MERs of mutual funds by going to the Globe Fund site on the Web at www.globefund.com.

You can compare the historic returns and MERs of mutual funds by going to the Globe Fund site on the Web at www.globefund.com.

Why Mutual Funds Cost More than Equities

Buying mutual funds is often more expensive than buying equity securities, even after factoring in commissions for buying and later selling the stocks. But it's important to remember that mutual fund shares are not ordinary securities. In effect they are a service contract entitling you to a unique package of securities and services not available with straight bond or stock purchases. These services include continuing professional management, diversification, ease of purchase and redemption, liquidity and a pro-rata ownership in the fund's net assets.

Closed-end Funds: Mutual Funds' Exchange-traded Cousins

So far we've talked only about mutual funds, or open-end investment funds, which are the most popular form of managed investments. There is another class of fund known as the closed-end investment fund, so called because the number of its shares or units outstanding often remains fixed.

Shares of closed-end investment companies are offered to investors at the time the fund is set up. Proceeds from this sale of equity are then invested in a diversified portfolio that is readjusted depending on market conditions. As with a mutual fund, a closed-end fund places its shareholders' money into investments that reflect the fund's particular policies and objectives. A closed-end fund is allowed to raise more capital by issuing debt securities. However, extra offerings of the fund's equity are either infrequent or not permitted by its charter, and the common stock isn't redeemed except in unusual circumstances, such as a tender offer, or when the fund is wound up.

There are about 40 closed-end funds in Canada. Unlike a mutual fund, whose shares are issued and redeemed by the fund itself, shares of closed-end funds trade on stock exchanges or on the over-the-counter market. Thus, when you buy shares in a closed-end fund, unless you are buying at the initial public offering, the purchase price goes to the seller of the stock, and doesn't contribute to the fund's own assets.

The market price of closed-end fund shares typically is at a large discount to the fund's net asset value. This discount reflects the market's view that the closed-end fund is a going concern that is unlikely to be wound up, with its paper assets realized at their then current break-up value.

Index Participation Units – Like Index Mutual Funds, But with Lower Costs

Index Participation Units (IPUs) are much like units of a mutual fund except that you buy and sell them on a stock exchange rather than from a fund company.

Canadian IPUs include i60s

If you invest in i60s, you are buying a share of a fund made up of the 60 companies in the Standard & Poor's/TSE 60 Index. The index is supposed to be representative of Canada's economy and the companies in it are among the biggest and most heavily traded in the country. These companies include Royal Bank, Canadian Pacific and Nortel Networks.

The i60s aim to track the performance of this index as closely as possible. That means you will never do better than the index. This is in contrast to most mutual funds, where a fund manager tries to beat a relevant index. However, most fund managers in the past have been unable to beat the indexes.

Each i60 unit is worth about 10% of the value of the S&P/TSE 60 Index. So if the index is trading at 500, a unit would be worth about $50. The trading symbol is XIU.

More details on i60s are available on the Web at Barclays Global Investors, www.iunits.com.

More details on i60s are available on the Web at Barclays Global Investors, www.iunits.com.

IPUs generally pay quarterly dividends, based on the dividends and other distributions the fund receives from the shares it holds. If the fund gets stock dividends, rights, warrants and other distributions from its holdings, it will sell them and distribute the cash to you, less fees and expenses.

Advantages of IPUs

The main attraction of IPUs compared to regular stock mutual funds is that they have lower yearly management costs. The management expense ratio (MER) on i60s is expected to be about 0.17%. This compares to more than 2% for the typical actively managed Canadian stock fund and around 0.5% to 1% or so for Canadian stock index funds. Stock index funds, like IPUs, are not actively managed and hold a basket of stocks designed to represent a particular stock index.

Because the stocks held by an IPU rarely will change, you always know what companies you own, while most mutual funds buy and sell investments regularly.

Another feature of IPUs is lower current-year capital gains taxes. Capital gains are kept to a minimum because the trust rarely sells its component stocks. An active stock fund manager, on the other hand, may do a lot of buying and selling – producing significant current-year taxes that you might instead prefer to delay. IPUs offer a wide range of trading options and flexibility. Unlike mutual funds, you can buy derivative contracts called options or futures on most IPUs. You can use these to either speculate on the IPU's future price direction or to reduce your risk by locking in a price ahead of a possible decline. You can profit from IPUs if their value drops since most qualify for short-selling, something you can't do with mutual funds.

Disadvantages of IPUs

IPUs will track downturns in the market. If the stock market falls, your return will drop along with it. The manager of an actively managed mutual fund, on the other hand, might be able to shift you into cash or take other defensive action to reduce your losses.

An IPU's returns are capped relative to the index; it can only do as well as the market benchmark, never better. An actively managed stock fund has the potential to beat the market, though most have been unable to do that consistently.

If you're an active trader or a short-term investor, it may be cheaper to switch in and out of mutual funds since you pay commissions to buy and sell IPUs.

And if you have only a small amount to invest, commission costs could make IPUs unsuitable. Mutual funds lend themselves to small purchases, and many don't charge a commission.

If you have only a small amount to invest, commission costs could make IPUs unsuitable.

You can't buy fractions of IPU units. So they don't work well in a dollar cost averaging program where you would invest a set dollar amount on a regular basis.

Other examples of IPUS

NASDAQ 100s

NASDAQ 100s give you exposure to the 100 U.S. stocks that make up the NASDAQ 100 Index. Companies in this index are typically newer technology firms. They include Microsoft and Amazon.com. The NASDAQ 100s trade on the American Stock Exchange under the symbol QQQ.

Each unit sells for about 5% of the value of the index. So if the index is at 4000, then one unit would trade for about $200.

This investment product pays dividends to unitholders quarterly, based on the cash distributions paid by the stocks in the portfolio, less fees and expenses. The MER is about 0.18%.

These units count as foreign content in an RRSP.

DIAMONDS

DIAMONDS, traded under the symbol DIA on the American Stock Exchange, are based on the well-known Dow Jones Industrial Average (DJIA). The Dow is made up of 30 blue chip stocks traded on the New York Stock Exchange.

The Dow Jones Industrial Average includes such companies as American Express, IBM, McDonald's, General Motors and Wal-Mart.

Units of DIAMONDS sell for 1/100th of the value of the Dow Jones Industrial Average. For instance, with the Dow trading at 10,000, each unit would trade at approximately $100.

DIAMONDS pay monthly dividends to unitholders based on the cash dividends paid by the stocks in the portfolio, less fees and

expenses. The MER on DIAMONDS is about 0.18%.
They count as foreign property in an RRSP.

SPDRs – Standard and Poor's Depository Receipts

Standard and Poor's Depository Receipts (SPDRs) are designed to track the performance of the broad S&P 500 Index in the U.S. This well-known index includes stocks like AT&T, Campbell Soup and Gillette.

They trade on the American Stock Exchange under the symbol SPY and are commonly known as "Spiders." Their price is roughly 10% of the S&P 500 Index. Assuming the S&P 500 Index is trading at 1,400, each SPDR would be about $140. Like stocks, they are traded throughout every trading day.

SPDRs investors are entitled to quarterly cash distributions corresponding to the dividends that accrue on the underlying stocks. Expenses are deducted from these dividends before investors get the distributions.

The MER is approximately 0.18%, far less than the average U.S. equity fund sold in Canada. They are considered as foreign content in an RRSP.

WEBS – World Equity Benchmark Shares

WEBS give you the opportunity to hold a representative basket of stocks for 17 different countries.

WEBS give you the opportunity to hold a representative basket of stocks for 17 different countries. Traded on the American Stock Exchange, the goal of each WEBS index series is to match the returns of the Morgan Stanley Capital International (MSCI) Index for the relevant country. Since the MSCI index measures a country's stock market activity, investing in WEBS can give you targeted exposure to a foreign country's stocks, without the need to make stock picks.

Each WEBS represents a broad underlying portfolio of publicly traded stocks in a particular country. Like foreign equity mutual funds, WEBS give investors exposure to international stock markets where it might otherwise be difficult to trade or even monitor holdings. All WEBS have three letters in their trading symbol, with the first two letters always EW. Germany WEBS is EWG. Japan WEBS is EWJ.

WEBS trade in U.S. dollars and each WEBS index series publishes its NAVPS daily following regular trading. This means the shares often trade at prices close to the basket's actual value. Net Asset Value (NAV) per WEBS for each WEBS index series is computed by dividing the value of the net assets of such WEBS index series by the total number of WEBS of such index series outstanding. Expenses and fees, including the management, administration and distribution fees, are accrued daily and taken into account for purposes of determining NAV.

Dividends and capital gains distributions are payable at least annually.

Here are the 17 WEBS currently available (with approximate MER in brackets): Australia (1.33%), Austria (1.68%), Belgium (1.24%), Canada (1.35%), France (1.52%), Germany (1.37%), Hong Kong (1.43%), Italy (1.33%), Japan (1.19%), Malaysia (1.46%), Mexico (1.63%), Netherlands (1.46%), Singapore (1.43%), Spain (1.67%), Sweden (1.64%), Switzerland (1.52%) and the United Kingdom (1.38%).

WEBS are classed as foreign property in your RRSP.

There are some possible complications you should remember about SPDRs, WEBS and DIAMONDS. The units of each trade in U.S. dollars. This exposes you to foreign currency risk if the Canadian dollar strengthens against the U.S. dollar. In the case of WEBS, there is an extra currency risk because the stocks in each portfolio will trade in their respective countries' currencies. Currency risk could wipe out gains you make in the foreign market if the currency goes against you.

You can get more information on SPDRs and DIAMONDS at the American Stock Exchange's Web site, www.amex.com. Details on WEBS are available at www.websontheweb.com.

Remember that dividends paid by SPDRs, WEBS and DIAMONDS don't qualify for the Canadian dividend tax credit. Any dividends these products pay are subject to a 15% U.S. withholding tax. However, you can claim a foreign tax credit for this on your income tax return.

SPDRs, WEBS and DIAMONDS can be held in your RRSP, subject to the foreign content restrictions.

You can get more information on SPDRs and DIAMONDS at the American Stock Exchange's Web site, www.amex.com. Details on WEBS are available at www.websontheweb.com.

Segregated Funds

These are a fund investment marketed with the promise of a "guarantee."

What you should know before you buy one of these, is that you are not completely covered against losing your money.

Key Characteristics

- A guarantee on your capital at two points in time: typically after 10 years or on your death
- Higher management fees than ordinary mutual funds
- May offer creditor protection
- If you die, money goes to beneficiary without probate fees

In most cases these funds – called segregated, guaranteed or protected funds – will only give you back your original investment after 10 years or on your death. If you withdraw your money in less than 10 years, you could lose money and get back less than you invested.

The chance of losing money in these funds is highest if you need to withdraw your money after just a short while. The risk diminishes the longer you hold the investment. That's because these funds are invested in stocks or bonds that fluctuate in value, which in turn affect the value of your investment in the fund.

Most of these funds are really just mutual funds with insurance policies attached.

As with mutual funds, there are ongoing costs you pay to the fund manager, including a fee to manage your money. These costs are known as the management expense ratio (MER). The MER on many seg funds is typically higher than for ordinary mutual funds. This reflects the extra cost for the insurance.

The insurance premium may add as much as 1% or more to the MER on an equity seg fund issued by a mutual fund company. Seg funds offered directly by insurance companies are typically less expensive and compare favorably with traditional mutual funds. However, a more variable cost are the sales commissions or "loads" insurance company seg funds charge. These have historically been higher than for regular mutual funds, and some seg funds still levy both a sales charge when you buy and a sales charge when you sell even though this practice has been abandoned by most of the fund industry.

Given the higher MERs and sales commissions for many seg funds, the question to ask yourself is do you need the insurance guarantee, and if you do, what price are you prepared to pay?

Likelihood of actually needing guarantee to get capital back after 10 years is small

Since stock markets have historically risen over the long term, the likelihood of actually needing the guarantee to get your original capital back after 10 years would be small. Consultants William M. Mercer found there's a 2% likelihood of losing money in the stock market over 10 years. Of course, this is no guarantee that history will repeat itself.

Reset option

Some companies selling segregated funds offer a "freeze" option. If your fund's value rises, you have the ability to lock in that new, higher value as the guaranteed amount. The guarantee date would then be reset to a new date 10 years down the road. So you would have to wait another 10 years to actually get that new guaranteed amount, although your beneficiary, of course, would collect sooner if you died.

The guarantee, depending on the policy, may be reduced to 80% or some other percentage once you reach age 90, for example. You can't buy some of these policies after you turn 80.

When the 10 years is up, you can leave your money in the seg fund, get your money out or convert it into an annuity.

The name "segregated fund" came about because the assets in the fund are held separately from the insurance company's other assets. Segregated funds are also referred to as "individual variable annuity contracts", or "variable insurance contracts".

If you die, the segregated fund, unlike other investments, goes to your beneficiary without your province charging probate fees. On the other hand, the higher management fees of seg funds may more than offset this advantage.

Segregated funds can give you protection from creditors, if the policy names an immediate family member as beneficiary. This may be particularly useful if you are self-employed. This protection may be lost if a court found you had set up the seg fund to avoid your debts.

Seg funds have traditionally been exempt from the rules that limit your RRSP's foreign content. However, most seg funds have actually stayed within this level. And anyway, seg funds held in an RRSP are to be covered by these limits starting in January 2002.

Protected funds are not considered to be insurance products. So probate fees are payable on them, and they don't offer creditor protection.

Wrap Accounts: The Investment Package with an all-in-one Fee

Wrap accounts are fee-based products which combine or "wrap" investment management, brokerage, custodial and reporting services into a flat annual fee based on the value of the managed assets.

Like a mutual fund, wrap accounts offer professional investment management.

These accounts were introduced to Canada in the early-1990s.

They allow more scope to tailor the holdings to your specific needs.

Wrap accounts are fee-based products which combine or "wrap" investment management, brokerage, custodial and reporting services into a flat annual fee based on the value of the managed assets. The fee would typically be an annual management fee of between 1.5 and 3% of the amount you have invested.

Your account statements might compare your returns to benchmarks like stock and bond indexes so you can see how your returns measure up.

Customized investment advice is a feature of both wrap accounts and also of traditional, full-service brokerage accounts. The assets in the wrap account may be individual stocks and bonds, pooled funds or mutual funds.

There are different types of wrap accounts:

- A mutual fund wrap uses mutual funds as its assets.
- Pooled wraps are similar to mutual fund wraps, but use pooled funds as their assets. You generally need at least $50,000 to get into these. The asset pool might be Canadian stocks, Canadian fixed-income securities, U.S. stocks and overseas stocks and fixed income investments.

Other wraps use individual securities – say stocks and bonds. The minimum investment in this case is usually about $150,000.

Another type lets you build your own portfolio in collaboration with your investment advisor. These also charge a fee based on asset size, with a certain number of "free" transactions included in that set fee. After a certain number of transactions, a fee would be charged.

Key questions to ask about wrap accounts include what you will get for the annual fee, whether you want and need this service, and how much are you willing to pay for it.

With a wrap account, the cost of a certain number of trades is generally included in the flat annual fee. This is an advantage, in the minds of some investors, because it removes a potential conflict of interest where your advisor might otherwise recommend trades because they generate a commission for the advisor – not necessarily because they benefit you.

Yet, there is probably not a financial advantage to you using a wrap account instead of a full-service brokerage account with mainly individual stocks and bonds. A commission-based account of $100,000 with a modest amount of trading would likely cost you less than either a wrap account or mutual funds, according to an analysis by the Investor Learning Centre of Canada.

Also, if you use a mutual fund wrap – by holding mutual funds in your wrap – you will be paying an extra set of fees. Canadian equity mutual funds, for example, charge annual management expense ratios that average more than 2% a year. If you hold these in a wrap account that charges say 2%, you will be paying 4% in combined management costs.

Another thing to watch out for with wrap accounts is the possible difficulty of leaving the wrap account. In some cases, the wrap account uses investments that are proprietary to the brokerage firm or mutual fund company. In this case, you may not be able to transfer the investments to another firm.

This means that if you wanted to switch brokerage firms or mutual fund companies, you may have to sell the investments. And this could create a substantial capital gains tax bill if the investments had good returns.

There are several variations on the wrap account. For one thing, some brokerage firms employ their own money managers to run the accounts. Others claim they attract better talent by contracting with independent managers.

Hiring Your Own Investment Counsellor

For those of us with a bit more money to invest, it's possible to get personal attention from your own private investment manager. How much money would it take? You'd probably need at least $1 million of investments to catch the ear of an established money manager, although half a million might be enough if a manager were looking to drum up business. With this money you would open a discretionary account.

Sometimes an ordinary investment advisor at a brokerage firm can act as a discretionary money manager for a client, but usually just for short periods of time, such as when the client is away on vacation. However, the investment advisor is prohibited from soliciting such business, and generally must clear all discretionary transactions with a director of the firm. When an investment advisor does solicit discretionary business from a client, he does so on behalf of the firm's money management department. Such accounts often are referred to as managed accounts.

Summary

There are several ways that you can use the talents of professional money managers. Buying mutual funds is one of them.

A mutual fund uses the money invested in it to buy a portfolio of securities. By owning units of a mutual fund, investors acquire a piece of that portfolio. Units are sold by the fund at that day's net asset value, plus any applicable sales charge. Investors wanting to dispose of their units sell them back to the fund, again at that day's net asset value. Whether you buy your units through an investment dealer or from a fund's own sales representative, you are buying new units from the fund rather than existing units from a selling investor.

Many people associate mutual funds with equities. This is only sometimes the case. There are many types of funds, each with its own investment objectives: bond, money market, balanced, equity, and global funds, to name a few. Each invests in particular asset classes. As well, fund managers employ differing types of investing styles. So even though buying a mutual fund means you are buying professional management, it still requires some investment knowledge to choose the fund that best matches your needs.

There are a number of fees associated with mutual fund ownership. With the exception of no-load funds, most funds have a sales charge, which can be paid either at the time of purchase or when the units are sold. In addition, investors pay a management fee, which is deducted from the fund's assets. Some funds collect other fees such as distribution fees, which are also deducted from the fund's assets. The total of all these fees is known as the fund's management expense ratio, and is expressed as a percent of its assets.

Mutual funds are also known as open-end funds because they are always issuing new units and redeeming existing ones from investors. A closed-end investment fund, on the other hand, has a fixed number of shares. Although it too uses the money it raises to invest in a portfolio of securities, it differs from a mutual fund in that its shares trade on a stock exchange, much like the shares of the companies in which it invests.

Index participation units are a cheaper alternative to actively-managed mutual funds. Segregated funds may offer you creditor protection.

With a wrap account, you pay a single all-inclusive fee – a percentage of your assets – to have your money managed by a professional. Some firms hire their own manager to look after these accounts, while others contract the work out to independent managers.

Getting into the Market

Become an experienced investor with the help of the right investment advisor.

In the last few chapters, you have had to grapple with some pretty difficult theoretical concepts about investing – such as what securities are and how the securities system works. Now, we get to relax a bit and talk about putting some of that theory into practice.

First of all, we'll outline the basic steps you should follow when you are getting into the market for the first time. Then we'll talk about the things you should continue to do as long as you remain in the market. You are going to find that we refer a lot to previous chapters. So feel free to look back if you need to refresh your memory on certain topics. After all, investing isn't a closed book exam – you get to peek as much as you like!

First Steps: Take Stock of Yourself

The first step towards getting into the market is taking stock of yourself. Everyone is different, and there's no way we can set out one way of investing that's going to be right for all investors. Some of us are conservative; we want to learn enough to invest intelligently with guidance from a professional investment advisor. Others are less averse to taking some risk and that might include doing your own legwork with a bit of help from the new investment and research tools available on the Internet.

Whatever your personal inclinations, there's room for every type of investor in the securities markets. But you have to think carefully about which type of investor you want to be, and what kind of investing you want to do. And you should think about this before you get started. Someone once said that the market can be an expensive place to find out who you are.

Whatever your personal inclinations, there's room for every type of investor in the securities markets.

For starters, you should ask yourself the classic financial planning questions. We're going to cover these in more detail in the next chapter. But just to give you a flavor of what we're referring to, here are some of the questions you need to answer before you begin investing.

How much money do you have to invest? What's your time horizon for investing? And what are your goals for the money?

Setting Goals is Essential

Now when we say goals, we mean something more specific than saying that you want to become a millionaire. For example, is safety of principal the most important thing to you? Or do you need to be able to get the money out quickly if you need it; that is, do you need a liquid investment? Are you trying to increase the principal you are investing – in other words, make a capital gain? Or are you looking for steady income? Then again, maybe you'd like the best of all worlds with a little of all of those things?

These questions deal with your financial situation and goals. They might sound complicated, but you should be able to come up with some straightforward, black-and-white answers with a little work. You can do this on your own with the aid of financial planning books or some of the forms we'll take a look at in the next chapter. Alternatively, you might want to consult a broker or financial advisor. We'll talk about this later.

Think about Your Tolerance for Risk

There are other questions you need to answer that require a little soul-searching. For instance, how much of a risk-taker are you? You can think of risk tolerance as a spectrum ranging from conservative to speculative, with varying shades in between. Where you lie in the spectrum will help determine the degree of safety that you should aim for when investing.

Your risk tolerance depends on your financial and personal situation.

But don't think of risk tolerance as just a personality quirk. It also depends on your financial and personal situation. Maybe for fun you like to skydive, ride fast motorcycles and bike to work in heavy traffic. But if you have limited financial resources, no pension plan and three children headed for college, it may not be a good idea to take a lot of risks with your savings. And maybe you should think about taking out some heavy-duty life insurance.

Another set of important questions has to do with the process of investing itself. What's your level of investment knowledge? And how much time do you want to spend thinking about your finances? Since you are reading this book, we'll assume you have some interest in financial matters, and that you are eager to learn. But even if you are all fired up about investing at the moment, think carefully about how much time and effort you'll be willing to spend in the future. Will you want to take the time needed to be an active, educated, self-directed investor? Or will you want some help in making financial decisions?

Choosing the Right Investment Advisor

If you see yourself needing some help, you'll be interested in the next step for the beginning investor – choosing an investment advisor. In Chapter 2, we talked about how the securities system works, including the role of brokers and investment dealers. As we mentioned then, the terms broker and dealer can be somewhat confusing. Technically, they are different. A broker acts as an agent, buying and selling an investment on behalf of the client, and getting a commission for the service. In contrast, a dealer buys an investment product with its own money and resells the product to customers.

The rules to become an IA in Canada are some of the most stringent in the world.

Another difference is that, traditionally, a broker or brokerage house tended to specialize in stocks, while an investment dealer focused on bonds. But today most investment firms trade both stocks and bonds, and can be referred to as either brokers or investment dealers.

Just to add to the confusion, the term broker is sometimes used to refer to both the investment firm – that is, the brokerage house – and to the people employed by the brokerage house to deal with clients. What's more, these people also can be referred to by other names, such as investment advisor, account representative, investment salesperson or registered representative. In our discussion, we will refer to the person you deal with at an investment house as an investment advisor – commonly called an IA.

How Investment Advisors are Qualified

The rules to become an IA in Canada are some of the most stringent in the world. An IA must be registered with the provincial securities commission to sell securities. Before you can be registered, you must pass the Canadian Securities Course, and an exam based on the Conduct and Practices Handbook, offered by the Canadian Securities Institute. New IAs must also undergo a 90-day training program provided by their companies. During those three months, IAs are barred from dealing with clients. After that, they are supervised closely and have to complete a demanding one-year financial planning course to remain licensed. Other qualifications may be required depending on the role that the IA performs, who they work for, and the products they sell. For example, to buy and sell options on behalf of clients, an IA must pass the Derivatives Fundamentals Course and Options Licensing Course offered by the Institute.

The Role of the IA

Now that we have a handle on what IAs are, let's talk about what they can do for you. IAs have two levels of responsibility. Their basic role is to trade securities on behalf of clients. When you want to buy stocks or bonds, you call your broker and place the order. Generally, the broker relays the order to the firm's trading desk, the trade takes place, and the broker takes care of any necessary paperwork. This includes sending you a confirmation of the trade, and updating your account. The firm also clears and settles the trade. That means making sure that you pay for the securities you buy, and that the person who sold them to you delivers the securities to your account.

Those are the essential order execution services provided by all investment houses. In addition, an IA working for a full-service firm will provide you with investment research and advice. Other brokerages choose not to provide clients with advice, and only execute clients' orders. These are called "discount" brokers, because they charge lower commission fees than full-service brokers.

Choosing the Right Broker

So when you start looking for an IA, the first thing you have to do is decide whether you want to use a full-service or discount firm. A discount broker is a good choice if you are a knowledgeable, experienced investor who knows exactly which financial products you want to buy and you have the time to devote to managing your investments. If you are interested in having help in making investment choices, however, a full-service firm may be a better choice.

Once you have made the decision about which kind of firm you want, you can begin your search. It's a good idea to choose a firm that's a member of one of Canada's Self-Regulatory Organizations (SROs) – the stock exchanges or the Investment Dealers Association of Canada (IDA). You can get lists of member firms from the exchanges or the IDA, or you can look in the telephone book. The SROs have minimum standards of conduct for their members, and jointly operate important industry organizations like the Canadian Securities Institute. The CSI not only educates the public, it also sets educational standards for brokers and others who operate within the SRO system.

The Canadian Investor Protection Fund

Another key organization is the Canadian Investor Protection Fund. The Fund protects clients in case a member firm goes under. If you have a general account with a brokerage house that's a member of an exchange or the IDA, your account is protected for up to $1,000,000 in cash and securities. You'll probably sleep better at night knowing that you don't have to worry about the financial health of the brokerage firm that's investing your money.

Canadian Investor Protection Fund protects clients in case a member's firm goes under.

Next, we'd suggest calling a few firms before making your

choice. Ask them if they are interested in your account. Ask about their commissions and fees. And if you are interested in a full-service firm, ask the branch or sales manager to recommend one or two brokers at the firm who would be good choices to handle your account. Then interview them. Your broker will have a big impact on your finances, so take the time to get to know him or her and decide whether this is the person for you.

What to Look For During a Broker Interview

Ask your broker about their education and experience as well as what their typical client is like.

You should start off by asking about their education and experience. The CSI has an advanced course, for example, called Canadian Investment Management. It deals with advanced wealth management techniques and portfolio management. If the broker has taken the course, it indicates a certain level of experience and knowledge that could be useful if you are looking for help with making sound investment choices. Some of the most experienced IAs have the letters FCSI after their names. This stands for Fellow of the Canadian Securities Institute, and it means the IA is somebody who has an exemplary track record and has met stringent educational requirements.

Also ask what the IA's typical client is like. If you were a senior citizen on a fixed income, for example, you'd have special needs. It might be reassuring to know that your broker has other clients like you. Some brokers may even specialize in meeting the needs of seniors, or of other segments of the investing public.

It's worthwhile to talk about mutual expectations, too. Discuss the services you are looking for, such as how often you want to be in contact. If you are not a active investor, it may be unrealistic to expect your advisor to call you constantly with research and recommendations. In fact, you would probably prefer that they didn't. But to make sure you are on the same wavelength, talk about it first.

Finally, before finalizing your decision to hire a particular IA, ask prospective IAs for the names and phone numbers of a few of their clients. Call these references and ask them about the strengths and weaknesses of each of these IAs.

The Know Your Client Rule

When you engage the services of an IA, you can expect a certain standard of service. There are numerous rules and regulations that advisors must follow. Most important is the cardinal rule guiding their behaviour – Know Your Client. Know Your Client means that the key focus of IAs must be suitability of investments. The IA must make a concerted effort to understand the client's financial and personal status and goals and only make recommendations that reflect these criteria.

That philosophy is reflected in the CSI's Conduct and Practices Handbook for Securities Industry Professionals. It says every member shall use due diligence:

- to learn the essential facts relative to every client and to every order or account accepted;
- to ensure that the acceptance of any order for any account is within the bounds of good business practice; and
- to ensure that recommendations made for any account are appropriate for the client and in keeping with his or her investment objectives.

This is the bottom-line behavior for an IA – and the minimum you should expect from your financial advisor.

As an investor, you too should make suitability your main focus. As we discussed earlier, before you start investing, you should consider your financial situation and your financial goals and think about the kind of investment products that would suit you. Then, when you are choosing an advisor, discuss your views on what you think are suitable investments. You and your IA should see eye-to-eye on your needs.

Opening an Account

So let's say you have found an IA who has the experience and knowledge to help you make suitable decisions. How does this important person find out what is suitable for you?

The main tool for IAs is the New Client Application Form

(NCAF) – the form you fill out when you first open an account with a brokerage firm. It's here that you must crystallize your financial objectives. This form provides the key information that will help your advisor choose suitable investments for you. It's in your best interest to make sure every fact on this application is as accurate and complete as you can make it.

The NCAF asks you a lot of questions, such as:

- Your full name
- Your permanent address, home and business telephone numbers
- Citizenship
- Occupation, employer, type of business
- If you are an officer, director or in a control position of a public company
- Age
- Investment objectives – risk tolerance
- Investment knowledge
- Net worth and earnings
- Bank and credit reference

Some of the questions may seem nosy – like your occupation or whether you are married. But this can be important in unexpected ways. For example, your occupation may indicate your level of understanding of the securities business. In addition, the identity of your employer could help guard against insider trading.

So don't be shy about telling your advisor the answers to these questions. At the same time, don't exaggerate facts, such as your income or level of investment knowledge or willingness to tolerate risk. If you do so, your IA might start recommending inappropriate investments. And that could get you into trouble.

Cash versus Margin Accounts

Your advisor will also ask you what type of account you want to open. The two main types of accounts are cash and margin.

If you open a regular cash account, you must make full payment for purchases or full delivery for sales on or before the settlement date. The settlement date for most securities is three business days after the trade.

On the other hand, if you open a margin account you'll be able to buy securities on credit. You'll pay only part of the full price at the time you make a trade. The part you pay, by the way, is called the margin. The brokerage firm will lend you the remainder, charging you interest on the loan.

Don't use margin unless you'll be able to come up with the cash to answer any margin call quickly and easily.

Buying securities on margin can be a good deal, and if you are an experienced investor you might want to explore this option. But there are pitfalls. When a brokerage firm lends you the money to buy securities, it uses the securities in your account as collateral. If those securities drop in price, the company may ask you to advance more money. This is known as a margin call and answering the call isn't optional. If you don't advance the money in time, the securities may be sold, possibly at a loss to you, to settle the account. So don't use margin unless you'll be able to come up with the cash to answer any margin call quickly and easily.

Whichever type of account you open, it's a good idea to talk with your broker about your responsibilities. Some of these are spelled out in a document known as a Client's Agreement, which will be sent to you when you open an account. For example, many agreements for both cash and margin accounts specify that the firm has the right to close out the account if proper settlement isn't made. Let's say you fail to pay in time for securities that you asked your advisor to buy. Under most agreements, the firm would legally be able to sell securities in your account to pay the outstanding balance. It's your responsibility to live up to the terms of the agreement.

One more thing – when you open an account with a firm, open a file of your own at home. Keep copies of every document that's important to you as an investor including your New Client Application Form, the Client's Agreement, and any statements sent by your advisor. It's a good way to keep on top of your investments. And if you ever have any problems, having the documents handy will help you find a solution much faster.

Starting to Invest

Prospectuses for Canadian public companies (and for mutual funds) can be downloaded from a Web site at www.sedar.com.

Opening an account is just the first step. Now you start the real business of being an investor – and that's investing, of course! First you have to decide what you want to buy. If you have done your financial planning homework, you should already know the types of investment suited to your needs. Now you have to narrow in on a specific investment. To do so, consult the many sources of information available to investors. These range from mass media like newspapers to detailed documents like annual reports and prospectuses. Most of these are available on the Internet or in print form. Prospectuses for Canadian public companies (and for mutual funds) can be downloaded from a Web site at www.sedar.com. Analyze the securities that interest you, using the techniques we discussed in Chapters 3 and 4. There are many other books and courses that teach methods to evaluate securities.

If you are dealing with a full-service investment house, you should ask your IA for research and recommendations. But don't feel obliged to act on all recommendations. Your broker has a responsibility to recommend investments that are suited to your needs. The final decision, however, is always up to you. Don't make an investment that you don't understand or that you don't agree with. Do your own thinking. If your broker is making recommendations that don't suit you, tell him or her how you feel. It's possible that your advisor hasn't understood your needs properly or that he or she has a different view on what's right for you. But if you have discussed the issue and you continue to disagree with recommendations, consider looking for another advisor.

Initiating the Trade

Once you have made an investment decision, it's time to put the trade into action. Let's say you want to buy a security. You call your broker and discuss the trade. There are four main pieces of information you'll need to specify: the name of the security; whether you want to buy or sell it; the quantity you want to trade;

and the type of order. The first two things are easy to convey to your broker. To identify a bond, you specify the issuer, the coupon and the maturity. For example, you might say that you want to buy the Government of Canada bond with a coupon of 9.75%, maturing in the year 2021.

To identify a stock, state the name of the issuer, and any specific details about the issue. Companies can issue more than one type of stock. For example, the Bank of Nova Scotia has both common and preferred issues. So be sure to tell your advisor exactly which one you want.

The Quantity

In addition, when you are trading a security, you should be aware that there are traditional ways to express quantities. If you are buying stocks, often the number of shares in an order is expressed as a "board lot." A board lot is a trading unit composed of a set number of shares. The number of shares in a board lot depends on the price. For stocks priced at and above $1, for instance, a board lot is 100 shares. So if you want to buy 1,000 shares of ACME and it's trading at $5, you would be looking at 10 board lots. On the other hand, for stocks that trade at under 10 cents on the Montreal, Toronto and Canadian Venture Exchanges, a board lot is made up of 1,000 shares.

A number of shares that is less than a board lot – say 50 shares of ACME – is referred to as an "odd lot". And a number of shares that can be expressed as a combination of a board lot and an odd lot – such as 450 shares – is known as a mixed lot.

Before you start trading, ask your broker to explain the terminology they use to express quantities of securities. And when you are giving an order, make sure there's no confusion about exactly how much you want. You don't want to end up with 1,000 shares of a stock when you really wanted 100 – or vice versa!

For bonds, the quantity is generally expressed in terms of the face value of the bond. If you have ever bought Canada Savings Bonds, you are probably familiar with this idea. For example, you might have bought one $1,000 CSB, or five $100 CSBs. It's the same with other bonds. A big investor, for instance, might buy a $100,000 Government of Canada bond with a 9.75% coupon, maturing in 2021. So if the price was, say 101.50, he or she would pay $101,500.

Types of Orders

Another part of your order you should think about is its type. The type of order can indicate several things, such as the price at which the trade will take place, and the time limit on the trade.

Market

In terms of price, the two main types of orders are market and limit orders. If you place a market order for a security, you'll pay, if you are buying, or get, if you are selling, the best price available at the time. An order that doesn't specify a price will usually be considered a market order.

Limit

If you place a limit order, you actually specify the price at which you are willing to trade the security. For instance, if you want to buy a security, you might set a price of $8 per share that you are willing to pay. Your order will only be executed if the market for that stock moves to that price or a better one.

Day

In terms of time, the two main types of orders are day and open orders. A day order is an order to buy or sell that is valid only for the day it's given. Say you tell your IA you want to buy 100 shares of ACME at a limit price of $8. The order can only be filled if the market price for ACME moves to $8 or better. If the order isn't filled by the end of the day, the order will be cancelled. It's important to note that all orders are day orders unless you tell your broker otherwise.

Open or Good Till Cancelled

An open order is also known as a Good Till Cancelled order. As the name suggests, this means your order will remain on the broker's books until it's executed or cancelled. However, many firms will limit an open order to a set amount of time – perhaps one month – and then remind clients about it. That way customers don't forget about an old order and then become surprised when it's suddenly executed.

Good Through Date

A customer can also specify a Good Through Date order. This is an order to buy or sell that is valid for a period specified by the client. As an example, you could give a limit order for ACME that is Good Through April 27. If it hasn't been filled by that time, the order is cancelled.

Any Part

There are many other types of orders that indicate the way a client wants a particular order handled. Generally, an order will be considered an Any Part order. That means if you have given an order for 100 shares of ACME at $8, but only 50 shares become available at that price, you'll end up buying those 50 shares.

All or None

However, you could specify that your order is an All or None order. Your order would have to be filled in its entirety on one day, or not filled at all. So if only 50 shares are available, your order would not be executed.

Fill or Kill

A Fill or Kill order states that as soon as part of the order is filled, the remainder is cancelled. If you want 500 shares of ACME, for instance, and only 100 are available at present, you would get those 100 shares, but the order for the remaining 400 would be cancelled.

Change Former Order

A type of order that could be important to you is the Cancel or Change Former Order. Always remember that if you have placed an order and it hasn't been filled either partially or totally yet, you have the right to cancel it or change it.

Either/Or

An Either/Or order means that the client puts in an order to buy or sell one security while another order or orders for other securities are waiting to be executed. As soon as one order is executed, the other is cancelled. Either one or the other is executed, but not both.

Contingent

A Contingent order is an order to buy one security and simultaneously sell another. For example, you might place a contingent order to sell 100 shares of ACME, and buy 100 shares of Zebra Corp. Contingent orders for two securities can be entered: a) at the market; b) at the same price; c) at a certain point spread; d) with a share ratio (e.g. 100 shares of ACME and 200 shares of Zebra). One side of the transaction cannot be completed without the other.

Switch

A Switch order is similar but not identical. It usually involves selling one security, and then using the proceeds to buy another.

Stop Loss

Another interesting type of order is known as a Stop Loss. This is an order to sell which becomes effective as a market order when the price of a board lot of stock declines to or below the stated limit or stop price. For example, if you bought Zebra shares at $10, you might decide to protect yourself by placing a stop loss order at $8. If Zebra shares declined to or below $8, your shares would be sold.

Hopefully your loss would be limited to about $2 a share. However, there's no guarantee of this, since your sell order would go into the market as a market order – meaning you'd try to get the best price possible at the time. That might be $8, or if the stock continued to decline, it might be less than $8.

Short Selling

There's another type of order that is fundamentally different from the rest. It's called short selling and it can be highly rewarding and dangerous. As we discussed in Chapter 5, a short sale occurs when you place an order to sell a security that you don't own. Your broker would borrow the shares for you from the firm's inventory or from another client. You might short sell if you believed that the price of the stock was going to fall, and you would be able to cover the sale by buying back the stock later at a lower price. For example, you might short sell ACME when it's trading at $8, and then buy it in the market when it's at $6. You would make a $2 per share profit. However, if the price of ACME had gone up, you would have lost money.

Just as with a regular transaction, you would have bought shares and sold shares, and your profit or loss would be the difference between the buy and sell prices. As usual, you would be trying to buy low and sell high. However, with short selling, the "sell high" comes before the "buy low".

The danger with short selling comes with the potential for loss. If you had bought a board lot of ACME at $8, for instance, the most you could lose – if the stock went to zero – is your entire $800 investment.

That's not the case with short selling. If you shorted a board lot of ACME at $8, the most money you could lose if things didn't go your way is impossible to know in advance, because we don't know how high ACME could go. But if you shorted ACME and then watched it climb to $20, you might have to buy it back at $20 and lose $1,200 – the $2,000 you would pay to buy it less the $800 you sold it for. This far exceeds the amount you invested, which in this case is the 50% margin requirement – $400 to start with and more as the stock climbed.

Of course, you wouldn't be compelled to buy the stock at $20. If you could meet the margin requirement and if you were patient, you might be able to wait out the upward move because there's no time limit on short selling. Unfortunately, there's no guarantee that ACME would ever go back down to $8.

At this point, you probably realize that short selling is a specialized technique that should be used only by knowledgeable and experienced investors. It's also something you must discuss thoroughly with your broker before doing. That's not just a suggestion. It's actually illegal for a seller not to declare that he or she is selling short at the time of placing the order.

For the moment, let's step back from the complicated world of special types of orders and pretend we're placing a run-of-the-mill order. Let's say you want to buy 10 board lots of Zebra Corp. You tell your broker the name of the company, the quantity, and the fact that you are willing to pay whatever price is going in the market. In other words, you are placing a market order.

If Zebra is an actively traded stock, your order may actually be executed within seconds, and your broker will confirm this over the phone. You'll also be sent a written confirmation.

Settling Your Account

The written confirmation will summarize the details of the trade, such as the quantity and the exact unit price at which the securities were traded. You should check it to make sure that the order was executed as you instructed, and that the information shown is correct.

For most securities, the settlement date is three business days after the day of the trade.

The investment firm's commission will also be listed. In the 1980s, a system of negotiated commissions was introduced in the Canadian stock exchanges, replacing the previous fixed schedule. You can shop around for the best rates. IAs usually charge a percentage of the order's value, depending on the order's size. There is also a minimum fee, so the commission on small orders may seem comparatively large. Discount brokers charge lower commissions, but as we mentioned earlier, do not offer any investment advice.

The written confirmation will also state the total amount that you owe the firm, if you bought stocks or bonds, or that the firm owes you, if you sold securities. As we mentioned earlier, if you have a regular cash account with your investment firm, you must make full payment for purchases or full delivery for sales on or before the settlement date. For most securities, the settlement date is three business days after the day of the trade. However, there are some exceptions. Bonds issued or guaranteed by the Government of Canada with a term of less than three years have two days to settle; and Government of Canada treasury bills settle the same day as the transaction. The settlement date is generally listed on the written confirmation. It's important to settle your account within the set settlement period.

Monitoring Your Investments

Once you have settled your first trade, you are officially a securities investor. Then the process starts all over again as you work to diversify your portfolio of investments.

Even if you are not actively accumulating more securities, you still have work to do as an investor. As long as you are invested in the capital markets, you must do several things: monitor your account; monitor your portfolio; and monitor your financial situation.

Be sure to read every statement, even if you haven't been trading recently.

Monitoring your account shouldn't be too difficult. In addition to sending you written confirmation every time you make a trade, your broker will send monthly statements detailing the activity in your account. If there is no activity in a month, no statement will be sent. You'll get quarterly statements, however, as long as you have cash or securities in your account.

Be sure to read every statement, even if you haven't been trading recently. If you don't understand what your statement shows, ask your advisor or another knowledgeable person to explain it to you. And if you ever see something in your account you don't agree with – say a trade you didn't authorize or another error – report it in writing immediately. If it's not corrected on your next statement, write to your IA and his or her supervisor again to tell them of the error. Most statements note that any discrepancies must be reported within a certain time frame, so it's important to address any problems immediately. Remember to keep copies of your statements and of every letter you send in your own financial file.

If writing a letter doesnít solve the problem, or it there are no written records to refer to, most problems can be solved within the branch. Should it be necessary, you can contact the Investment Dealers Association, assuming, of course, that your account is with a member firm. The IDA can investigate your situation and get to the bottom of it. They can require a member to submit background information or attend a hearing. Problems in the industry usually don't have to go this far to get resolved, but it's good to know that the process is there if you need it.

In addition to monitoring your account, monitor the securities that make up your portfolio. You already know that you should do a reasonable amount of research and thinking before you buy a security. And you shouldn't stop once the trade is made. The company in which you invested may change, or the economic situation may change. Periodically review each security to make sure it's right for you.

Keeping Track of Your Financial Situation

Of course, to do this properly you also have to monitor your own financial situation. Your own status and goals may change in a way that makes a security no longer suitable for you. And if circumstances do change, don't just keep it to yourself. Remember to tell your IA. If you should experience a big change in your net worth or annual income – hopefully for the better – tell your investment firm. Your IA bases his or her recommendations on the facts known about you. So make sure they are right.

Finally, monitor the securities business and the capital markets. What you have learned in this chapter is a good starting point. But there's plenty more to know. Continued learning about the market is the best investment you'll ever make.

Using an online broker

There are definitely some positives in online trading for the small investor. The two big advantages are cheap trading and convenience.

But you must remember that successful investing is all about the amount of time you spend in the market – not market timing. The ability to make quick trading decisions based on short-term information is a big pitfall of online trading. You could find yourself making highly speculative investments if you're not careful. It's important to do the same amount of research you normally would if you weren't trading online. Don't let the convenience of online trading lull you in to forgetting to do your homework. Know what you are investing in before you click the submit button.

Don't let the convenience of online trading lull you in to forgetting to do your homework. Know what you are investing in *before* you click the submit button.

To open an account on the Internet, most brokerages require you keep at least $1,000 in your account. Some firms set a minimum of at least $20,000.

Then the brokerage will send you a Personal Identification Number (PIN) and a user name. This lets you log onto their Web site. At their site, you can look at your portfolio, check to see how much money is in your account and review your account's trading history.

You may have access to various research tools such as company news releases and charts. Some brokerages offer you third-party information from Financial Post Data Group, Standard and Poor's or Baseline. Or the brokerage might have its own proprietary research available to you on its Web site. Several also offer mutual fund research tools.

Entering orders to buy stocks or mutual funds is straightforward. You complete a form online and submit it to the brokerage firm at any time of the day or night. But the execution of your order will generally be done during regular trading hours.

Once your order is received, an Investment Representative will check to see that what you want to buy is consistent with your objectives. You should get an immediate e-mail message showing that your order was in fact received. Then, if your order is approved, it will be sent on to the relevant stock exchange or mutual fund company. When the order is actually filled, you will get an electronic confirmation from your brokerage's Web site. A written confirmation will also be mailed to you.

Pointers for trading online:

- Even though online trading is quick and easy, online investing takes time. Your mouse might let you make a trade in a nanosecond. But wise investment decisions take time. Before you trade, know why you're buying or selling, and what the risk is;
- Because of the risks of borrowing to invest, consider spending only the actual cash that you have in your account. Some brokerages will let you spend more than your cash balance – through a margin account;
- Remember you have three business days to pay the brokerage: if you don't, they can sell some of your securities to recover their money;
- Use time in the market – not market timing – to guide your investing;
- If you are buying a highly volatile stock, consider placing a limit on the price you are willing to pay by using a limit order. Just because you see a particular price on your computer doesn't mean that's the price you will always get. You should submit an order to buy at a specific price, or less. If the price jumps, you won't buy the stock – and won't end up paying much more than you expected;
- Know your options for placing a trade if you can't get access to your account online. Most online brokerages offer alternatives for placing trades, such as touch-tone phone trades, faxing your order – or the old-fashioned way, by phoning a real-live person. Check to see if these options may increase your costs. Don't forget that if you experience delays getting online, you may have similar delays using the alternatives;
- If you place an order, don't assume it didn't go through. Investors sometimes mistakenly assume their trade orders weren't

executed and submit another order. They end up either owning twice as much stock as they intended, or selling stock they didn't own. Check with your firm on what procedure you should follow if you are unsure if your original order was executed;

- If you cancel an order, make sure your cancellation went through before you place another trade;
- Remember that no regulations require a trade to be executed within a certain time. Firms may advertise a certain speed of execution, but delays do happen;
- The range of trading orders you can use online varies, depending, on the particular discount broker you use. So you should check before you decide which discounter to use. Some discounters don't allow the full range of orders;
- Treat online investing as a convenience and as a cost-saving tool – not as a short-term trading tool or as a way to speculate.

Using the Web to research companies and industries

The Internet offers a wide range of information for investors doing research. Here are some suggestions:

Brokerage research

Full-service brokerage firms, and, increasingly, discount brokers, offer reports that examine industries and the companies operating in these industries. The reports offer earnings estimates and recommend whether the stocks of particular companies in these industries should be bought, sold or held. They are generally available at no cost to clients of full service brokerages. Discount brokerages typically charge a fee.

Check the latest news in a particular Canadian industry by selecting the industry (or company) of your choice at Carlson Online at www.carlsononline.com.

On the Web, brokerage research reports on industries and companies in Canada and the U.S. are available on a per-page or per-report basis at typically $5 to $150 (U.S.) per report. You can get these reports through sites such as Yahoo finance at http://finance.yahoo.com and www.northernlight.com which links to the Investext Group's reports that are prepared by various brokerages. Research reports on U.S. and Canadian companies, which include industry information, are available from Zack's Investment Research at www.zacks.com. Reports from this site start at $10 (U.S.) per report.

Check the latest news in a particular Canadian industry by selecting the industry (or company) of your choice at Carlson Online at www.carlsononline.com.

Sedar has annual reports of Canadian public companies and mutual funds

Annual reports – and other regulatory filings by Canadian publiccompanies – can be viewed and downloaded off the Internet from the Canadian Securities Administrator's site at www.sedar.com. SEDAR stands for System for Electronic Document Analysis and Retrieval. The Canadian Securities Administrators – the umbrella organization of Canada's provincial securities commissions – have told public companies and mutual funds that they must send their regulatory filings to this site. This means you've got access to disclosure documents like financial statements, prospectuses, annual reports and annual information forms at one Web site.

These documents are a free wealth of information about stocks, mutual funds and other securities. Learn about the risks of these investments – and what the costs are – by reading this information before you consider buying. You'll also find news releases that have been issued by the companies and mutual funds.

Before thinking of buying a company's stock or a mutual fund's units, make sure you check certain things that likely won't be available on the SEDAR site. You will want to know the current and recent share or unit price of the stock or fund, and the earnings history. This information is available at various Web sites, including The Globe and Mail's Globe Investor at www.globeinvestor.com.

Want to find out about a particular company? You can do a search on SEDAR for all the documents filed by the company. Maybe you only want to look at its latest prospectus. You can confine your search to that type of document. Or you can do a search for, say, all documents filed by that company for a time period that you set.

Companies are also listed by letter of the alphabet. So if you want to look up, say, Shaw Communications, take a look under "S".

Maybe you want to research companies in the broadcasting industry. SEDAR organizes companies under 68 industry categories. So click on "broadcasting" and then do searches of all the public companies in that one industry. Decide what type of documents you want, and tailor your search accordingly.

A company's annual report offers a range of information about the company – including whether it is making any money and how much debt it has.

In the management's discussion and analysis section of a company's annual report, you should find an overview on conditions or trends in the company's industry.

Mutual funds have their own section on the SEDAR site. You can search by fund company, time period, and by type of report.

Most documents on SEDAR can be read only if you have software called an Adobe Acrobat reader. You can download that software for free from the company's Web site at www.adobe.com.

Some of the documents on SEDAR are hundreds of pages. You don't have to wade through every page. Instead, check the table of contents at the start of the document to find the sections that interest you. Jot down the page numbers and then use the Adobe page-count feature on the lower left of your screen to skip ahead to the pages you want to check.

Looking for particular words or phrases? There's an easy way to do this: use the "binoculars" icon on the toolbar at the top of your Adobe screen. Just click on the icon and type in the word or phrase you're after. Then let the computer search the document for you.

For regulatory filings of U.S. companies and mutual funds, check SEDAR's American equivalent at the Edgar Web site, www.edgar-online.com.

Industry Canada Web site

You can find a whole host of statistical information on various industries – including comparisons with the particular industry's U.S. counterpart – at this site. There are details on employment and production, trade and who the major industry players are. The site includes an overview on different industries. You can download information free. The Web site address is www.strategis.ic.ca.

Statistics Canada Web site

Statistics Canada offers a range of general information on various industries at no charge. The data includes the annual supply and demand for particular products in recent years. To get all data available on a particular series, or for a more detailed series, there's a $3 fee. The Web site is www.statcan.ca.

Economic forecasts and analysis by the banks

The banks offer general reports outlining economic and industry trends in newsletters. These are generally available at the branches and from the banks' Web sites at no cost.

Industry associations

Industry associations often conduct surveys and commission research into changes and issues facing their industries. Much of this information is posted on their Web sites, along with industry news and links to other information sources. Check the Industry Canada site at www.strategis.ic.gc.ca for information about industry associations and trade publications.

Trade shows

To better understand the dynamics of an industry, professional analysts often attend industry trade shows to talk with company representatives and to see new products and projects first hand. Trade shows are a good opportunity to speak to employees of the company you're interested in, as well as to gain insights from people at competitor firms.

Check the Industry Canada site at www.strategis.ic.gc.ca for dates and locations of these shows, organized by industry sector.

Summary

Before you enter the market, do some self-examination. Try to quantify your time horizon, the money you have available, the level of risk you can live with, and your investment objectives.

Then you should choose an investment dealer and an IA. This is an important decision, so talk to a few candidates before deciding. You then fill out the New Client Application Form and open an account. A margin account lets you borrow part of the cost of the securities you buy, whereas with a cash account you are expected to pay for your purchases in full.

You then must decide what to buy. Your IA will make suggestions and provide you with research reports, but you make the final decision. The IA will advise you on how much to buy and what type of order to use. Experienced investors who think that a stock is going to decline in value can execute a short sale, which will be profitable for them if the stock does decline.

After paying for the transaction, your next task is to monitor your account and your investments. Check the accuracy of the statements the investment dealer sends you. Regularly review the prospects of the companies you have invested in. Review your own financial position, and notify your IA of any changes. Finally, keep learning about the investment markets.

Online investing is a convenient and low-cost way to trade. You can research investments using the Internet, too.

Financial planning

Putting your investment knowledge to work.

So far, we've touched on just about every aspect of investing. Now it's time to fit all of this information together and make sure your investment decisions help you get where you want to go. The best place to start is at the beginning – by drawing up your financial plan. And the first step is to define your own goals and objectives and prepare a budget. Once you have these basics out of the way, you can then begin the investment process.

Unfortunately, while most Canadians have investments in one form or another, few of us set aside our savings or buy and sell securities according to a comprehensive financial plan. Most of us may want to be rich, but few of us map out a strategy for realizing our dreams. Fewer still are able to stick to it year after year.

Maybe that's why lottery tickets sell so well – because most people have failed at their financial planning. The dream of winning is the ultimate quick fix, but it's not a safe bet. Financial independence does not occur by luck but rather by choice.

The Financial Plan

To start the process, you should recognize that a good plan contains several basic characteristics. It must: 1) be do-able, 2) accommodate the bumps and grinds of daily life, 3) be simple enough to follow and 4) provide for life's necessities as well as some luxuries. It will, by design, be a personal and unique strategy for you and your family. This will not be an easy process, as there are key decisions to be made along the way.

Start at the Beginning

The first thing you must do when starting to construct a financial plan is to record your current situation. We're providing some sample forms you can use for this purpose. First, you should fill out a Financial Information form. List all financial institutions you deal with: investment dealers, financial planners, mutual fund companies, banks, trusts, and credit unions as well as insurance agents. Account numbers and contact people should be listed clearly; you may not be around to explain things to someone else. The name and contact information for your lawyer, accountant and doctor should be recorded.

Because either your family or your executor might use this information, make it clear and concise. List the location of all key papers including passports, previous years' tax returns, wills, insurance policies, mortgage documentation, property deeds, and loans and IOUs. List the location of your safety deposit box and its keys. But most importantly, tell someone, such as your spouse, that you have made this list, and where to find it.

Measuring Net Worth

A statement of your current net worth is a strategy point to measure how well you are doing when it comes time for review.

Next, prepare a statement of your current net worth. This is really just a simple balance sheet that will concisely show you how much money you have, or don't have, as the case may be. It's a snapshot picture really, valid only on the day it's calculated; but you must have a starting point to measure how well you are doing when it comes time for review.

Calculating Your Income

Now comes the income statement. Once you have calculated your income, work out your expenses and see what is left over. This balance is what you can invest. If the amount isn't significant, try reworking your budget to see if you can increase the investment part. Once you reach what you think is the maximum amount, consider the investment spectrum. We'll get to it later.

This might seem like a complicated task, but the records you need should be readily available if you get into the habit of holding on to them. You'll need to refer to your T4 slip for employment income, plus your pay stubs if your income varies significantly over time – for example, if part of your earnings comes from commissions. Also hold on to any other record of income such as interest or dividend income from any investments you already have.

Tracking Your Expenses

Figuring out your expenses should be fairly straightforward. Examine all your regular bills such as gas, hydro, cable, telephone, property tax and insurance. Check your bank statement for any automatic withdrawals. Don't just refer to a single bill for your estimate, as some of these expenses will fluctuate significantly from month to month. Try to keep track of food, entertainment and miscellaneous household expenses for a month or two to see exactly where the money goes. And remember to check your credit cards for routine purchases.

Some people use a computer-based system to keep track of their investments and budget. This is appropriate if you are computer literate and, of course, if you have a computer. There are some excellent financial software products available, some for well under $100. Whatever system you choose, think about it carefully. Will you consistently maintain your computer-based records or is such a system more trouble than it's worth?

The Life Cycle Approach to Financial Planning

Once you know where you are financially, you can develop a plan. It can be useful to start with an overview of the five stages of an adult's financial life. That way, you can see where you fit in, and have some idea of what lies ahead.

Phase One – Starting Out

This first phase begins after the college or university years. Most people start their first job and move into their first apartment. It's the beginning of a career and could entail a lot of capital spending on mundane household items. There are few responsibilities; it's a time of testing your wings and learning. Cash inflow is meagre while cash outflow is usually large. This is an easy time to get into financial trouble through overspending. A key word at this stage could be "budget".

Phase one is time for adventure and speculative trading fits this adventure-some spirit.

While it may be difficult at this stage to save, a portion of income should be set aside, if only to introduce discipline into your life. Big purchases should not be made on credit. In terms of investments, Guaranteed Investment Certificates may be too boring, while option and commodity trading may have more appeal. This is a time for adventure, and speculative trading fits in with this adventuresome spirit. Risks should not be open-ended though and should be limited to an affordable amount. That means no short selling. But while emotionally you may be ready and willing to speculate, there's usually one small problem – lack of funds. A savings plan could be used to accumulate funds for risky investments. At this point in one's life a high-risk security could be attractive if only from a learning point of view. It's probably the most appropriate time for such speculative trading because losses will not affect retirement planning drastically at this point in time. As well, any losses that do occur with speculative trading will have a sobering influence on the young investor.

This isn't to say that people start their investing lives by going on a speculative binge. It always makes more sense to start slowly. As you gain experience and knowledge, you can move on to more complex and speculative investments. You could even conceive of a knowledge cycle that works differently than the life cycle: you start out at the conservative end of the investment spectrum. As you acquire more knowledge and, not incidentally, more assets, you begin to branch out and take on more risk. You work toward a diversified portfolio with a mix of investment products and risk levels.

Pay Yourself First

Of course, it's hard to get started if you have no money to invest. That's where a regular savings plan comes into the picture. Too many of us pay for life's expenses as they come at us with the intention of socking away any money that happens to be left over at the end of each month. Unfortunately, it's just too easy to spend whatever we are able to spend. The key is make sure that something as critical as savings doesn't end up in your wallet as discretionary income.

That's why the habit of paying yourself first – of considering your savings as a bill that cannot be ignored – is so key. It simply means that out of every paycheque, including bonuses and commissions, if you are lucky enough to be paid in this way, comes a certain dollar amount or percentage. This isn't easy when your income is low and there are so many things you may need or want, so many things to buy. But by taking even $50 out of each paycheque, you begin to build a small reserve of money for emergencies and big-ticket items. If you start now and think of such savings as a bill to be paid, like rent or cable or other regular monthly payments, you can start yourself on the road to good financial health. The easiest way to accomplish this pay-yourself-first technique is to arrange an automatic withdrawal from your chequing account into a savings account. Some people find is easier if they actually write a cheque for deposit to their savings account; others open this savings account at an out-of-the-way branch so there's less temptation to raid the account for everyday spending. Alternatively, you can set up a monthly savings plan with a mutual fund company. Funds are withdrawn from your bank account and used to purchase units in a money market or short-term income fund. You know yourself best – set up the savings plan in a way that suits your personal habits.

Using Credit Wisely

It's important to start building a credit rating at this point, but often the temptation of a credit card is simply too much for the person just starting out. If you get into the habit of using a credit card now, you could be establishing some bad habits, habits that are difficult to break. Of course, if you do need a credit card you must learn to use it wisely. Here are some tips to follow:

- Choose a credit card that can accomplish most of the transactions you'll make on credit. Holding five or 10 different cards may look impressive, but it's much easier to lose track of what you have spent if there are many separate bills coming into the house.

- Stick to a preset credit limit – decided by you. A credit card company isn't in the business of giving you credit for your convenience. They want you to owe money so they can charge you interest. There's a fine line between making your payments regularly and overspending. If you feel you can manage a $500 limit and only that, choose that limit. Often if you are punctual and pay off your bills regularly, a company will raise your limit. It sounds like an honor to be offered a $5,000 limit, but it's in fact foolish unless your cash flow is such that you can and will pay off such an amount at the end of the month. That's the key – set your limit at what you can afford to pay off in full each month.
- Shop around for the best deal. Like most financial services now, there are a variety of credit cards to choose from, even among the same carriers. Decide what you need the card for, work out your credit limit as well as the number of times you intend to use the card per month, and then compare the different packages available. Cost will be a key determinant.
- Pay off the outstanding balance every month. Better yet, set aside the money when it's charged. That way there will be no squirming at the end of the month to meet the payment.

Above all, remember that credit is like gambling – it's addictive. It's easy to live the good life on credit, until it catches up with you.

You should be aware that credit cards are not the only type of credit you'll encounter as a consumer. Many retailers have those special "Buy now, pay later" promotions. It's not free credit though. The cost of lending you that money is built into the price of the item you are purchasing. A retailer is in business to make money, so there are no free rides. It's not the retailer's fault or problem if a consumer overspends.

Even if the cost of delaying your payments isn't built into the product, you can still end up getting into trouble. Let's say you want a new car and you arrange to buy it now and start paying for it in six months. Instead of buying a $15,000 car, you move up to a car worth $17,500 because you'll save the first six months of car payments, and, of course, you'll put that money aside in the meantime. What really happens is that you spend the money on something else and still ending up owing the extra $2,500, so now you are out $5,000. This may not seem like a lot, but unless you are disciplined about your spending and saving habits, it's easy to accumulate debt.

Phase Two – Marriage, Mortgage, Children

The late twenties to early forties phase is characterized by a series of important milestones. This is the time of our lives that usually includes getting married, buying a house and starting a family. Investors tend to be more adventurous at this stage but more responsibilities are being taken on. Work or job-related activities take on more importance, and leisure time activities tend to be replaced by house maintenance and family outings. Switching from freedom mode to family mode brings financial responsibilities and constraints.

Those who have started their $50 per paycheque plan may now have greater difficulty in saving, as there's always a new lawnmower, air conditioner or other household expense popping up. In fact, what little has been saved may already be spent. But maintaining this type of plan is more important than ever, if only for vacations and emergencies. Maintaining the discipline of saving regularly is vitally important as well.

Savings can be invested in various ways, although, for most, a high degree of liquidity is necessary to cover emergencies and other contingencies. Speculative investments are usually not liquid, and any speculating should be viewed as an expense rather than an investment. You must accept upfront that there may be no return on your money and no return of the money invested. It has to be money that will cause little or no hardship if lost.

It's also time to start saving for your children's education. Whether or not one chooses a Registered Education Savings Plan, putting money away now when the children are young will certainly mean that paying for college or university later on does not break the bank. Alternatively, you should at least plan to have your mortgage paid off before the oldest child graduates from high school. That way, you'll have more room to take on educational expenses.

If you haven't started saving money on a regular basis yet, it's not too late to start. These habits should be well developed before moving into the next phases of the life cycle, when retirement and investment savings become more important than ever before.

Here again, using cash instead of credit whenever possible is key. While credit like a credit card, line of credit or overdraft protection at your banking institution are often necessary, you should avoid using this protection if you can.

This isn't to say that credit is inherently evil. The fact is, just about everyone but the independently wealthy will need credit at some point in their lives. How could most of us afford to buy a home without it? You might also need credit to buy a car so you can get to work or to tide you over during temporary cash flow problems if the furnace goes kaput in the middle of winter. The key word here, however, is temporary. The problem with credit is that far too many people rely on it as a way to live beyond their means indefinitely.

Phase Three – The Core Years: Moving Up Financially

The years from 40 to 55 are peak income years, but they could also be the most difficult. Mid-life crisis, depression, divorce and other personal problems are most likely to occur in this phase. The mortgage may be paid off and the children finishing college, but there can also be a possibility of job loss. This period of life often becomes a time for taking stock, as people look back over their lives to see what accomplishments and goals have been reached. For some, career changes or financial upheavals can occur. Stress can be a big problem. Added to all that is a growing sense of mortality.

With a lot of the financial responsibilities such as children's education expenses and a mortgage paid off, this may be the first opportunity that most people have to really save money for investment and retirement purposes. One of the biggest mistakes made at this point is taking too much risk in an effort to make up for lost opportunities. This is unwise. Investments should be reasonably conservative, with speculation taking a back seat. Money should increasingly be put aside for retirement purposes into Registered Retirement Savings Plans and company pension plans.

RRSPs – The Best Way to Save for Retirement

Without a doubt, RRSPs are the best investment vehicle available to the average Canadian. Introduced by the federal government in 1957, RRSPs contain powerful tax incentives designed to encourage us to save for our own retirements. Each year, you are entitled to contribute up to 18% of your earned income into an RRSP, subject to a maximum annual contribution of $13,500*.

The effect on your tax bill can be tremendous. Let's say your earned income is $40,000, so your RRSP contribution limit is 18% of this figure or $7,200. If you did contribute $7,200 to your RRSP, your taxable income would be reduced from $40,000 to $32,800. So the $7,200 is a tax deduction. As well, your contribution is tax sheltered within the plan. That means that as this investment appreciates or earns income, no tax is payable. Instead, tax is payable when you withdraw money from the plan, which you must do no later than the year you turn 69. Withdrawals from an RRSP are taxed at your then current rate of income tax. Or, you can roll over the contents of your RRSP into a Registered Retirement Income Fund or RRIF, which will continue to shelter your money.

**This amount is reduced by any contributions made by you or your employer to a registered pension plan or group RRSP if you have one. We'll have more to say on this subject later.*

Government Pensions Aren't a Sure Bet

One of the reasons RRSPs have become so popular in recent years is the increasing uncertainty surrounding government retirement benefits. Unlike many private pension plans, the Canada Pension Plan and other federal retirement benefits are not pre-funded.

Old Age Security has been scaled back or eliminated for all but the lowest income earners and CPP premiums have begun to rise dramatically.

Instead, they meet their obligations through general tax revenues. So far, this arrangement has worked because of the high proportion of working age taxpayers in comparison to retirees. But what will happen to these benefits by the time the baby boom generation retires? Will a smaller work force be willing to carry the tax burden required to fund the benefits all those seniors expect to get? The answer is probably no. Indeed, we have already seen signs that the current scheme is unsustainable. Old Age Security has been scaled back or eliminated for all but the lowest income earners and CPP premiums have begun to rise dramatically.

Employer-sponsored Pension Plans

If you are lucky enough to be working for a company that has a pension plan, you are definitely at an advantage. However, you should carefully read the plan documents so you can understand exactly what you can expect to get in the future. There are basically two types of plans.

The defined benefit plan guarantees a certain income at retirement. To make sure you get that promised benefit, the plan sponsor hires actuaries who decide the amount of money that has to be directed toward the plan over time. Your ultimate benefit is based on a formula. This may be the number of years of plan participation times a certain percentage. For example, a 30-year employee in a plan that pays 2% for each year of service will get a retirement benefit equal to 60% of their working income.

In contrast, the other main type of pension plan – defined contribution – doesn't promise any set amount at retirement. It defines your contributions and those of your employer, but everything else is variable. Your ultimate retirement income will depend on the level of contributions during your years in the plan, the choices you make in the way those funds are invested and the performance of those funds over time. In recent years, employers have tried to phase in defined contribution plans wherever possible because they are budgetable in advance and avoid much of the expense and red tape associated with defined benefit pension plans. In fairness, it should be pointed out that many younger employees, especially those who are inclined to move between jobs during their careers, prefer to have more immediate control over their retirement savings.

If you belong to a defined benefit plan, you should get a document annually from the plan's administrators describing your expected income level at retirement, given your current level of contributions. If you belong to a defined contribution pension plan or group RRSP, you should be able to make a reasonable estimate based on the factors we just described. Remember, though, that your projections will be more accurate if your pension contributions are invested in a GIC or mortgage fund rather than Canadian equities.

The Pension Adjustment

No matter what type of registered pension plan you belong to, your RRSP contribution limit will be adjusted downward in an effort to equalize the opportunity for tax-assisted savings between all taxpayers. In other words, Revenue Canada wants to give all taxpayers – whether they are fortunate enough to be covered by a private pension plan or not, the same overall limit for tax-deductible retirement savings contributions. Thus, the government calculates a Pension Adjustment or PA to reflect the current value of contributions to your pension plan and that amount is subtracted from your RRSP contribution limit. This information is sent to you by the government with your notice of assessment from last year's tax return. Some taxpayers complain that they are penalized with a lower RRSP limit simply because they happen to be members of a pension plan. However, they are still way ahead of taxpayers who do not belong to pension plans and thus have to fund their retirements without the contributions of an employer.

It Pays to Start Early

Whether you combine a pension with an RRSP for your retirement or only use an RRSP, start your contributions early. And if you can afford it, put in the total allowable contribution, and the one-time $2,000 allowable over-contribution. Although the over-contribution

Remember that unused contribution room can be carried forward into subsequent tax years and used when you have the money to invest.

isn't tax deductible, it's still allowed to grow tax-sheltered without penalty. And it may be deductible at some point in the future when you do have extra contribution room. You should remember that unused contribution room can be carried forward into subsequent tax years and used when you have the money to invest.

RRSP Investment Options

Some people believe that an RRSP should only include fixed-income securities such as GICs. We disagree. If you have a large investment portfolio that extends outside the RRSP, it makes sense to have your fixed income portion tax sheltered, since fixed-income investments attract a higher tax rate than capital gains. But if your investment portfolio is limited, some growth or equity exposure is appropriate within the RRSP, especially if you have quite a few years to go until retirement, and thus time to ride out any fluctuations in the stock markets. What's more, if you just invest in fixed income you could become a victim of inflation.

Once you have an idea of what type of plan interests you – from GICs to equities – you can choose between a managed plan like a mutual fund, or a self-directed plan. You can buy either type through most brokers, banks and trust companies. You can also buy an RRSP directly from a mutual fund company, although you would be limited to that particular company's funds.

You can have as many RRSPs as you want. But remember that it pays to keep things simple. Ten or 15 different plans may become a bit of a headache and could be costly, too, if each plan charges a trustee or administration fee.

Self-directed RRSPs

If you have confidence in your investment ability and the inclination to take a more active role in your finances, the self-directed RRSP offers quite a bit more flexibility than off-the-shelf RRSP products. A self-directed RRSPs is a personal, all-inclusive retirement savings account. It can contain just about every type of security imaginable including GICs, mutual funds and individual stocks and bonds and in some cases, even your own mortgage. The broker, bank or trust company that keeps track of your assets will send you a monthly account statement that offers a handy snapshot of your investments and makes it easy to monitor performance.

The cost of all this convenience is small – about $100 a year or nothing at all depending on the size of your account.

The Foreign Content Limit

You can diversify your RRSP by holding a certain percentage in foreign investments. The foreign content limit for 2000 is 25%, and for 2001, 30%. It's based on the book value of the investments; that is, what you paid for them. This usually requires a self-directed RRSP. Your plan administrator keeps track of the value of your domestic and foreign investments and will usually advise you when you are in danger of contravening the limits. But you should keep an eye on this.

Borrowing from Your RRSP

In recent years, the government has tried to encourage home ownership by making it possible for taxpayers to borrow money from their RRSPs towards the down payment on their first house. There are limits on who can participate and to what degree, and it does reduce your contribution limits.

Self-directed RRSPs have the flexibility to hold the mortgage on your own house.

RRSPs have the flexibility to hold the mortgage on your own house, although you have to treat the loan as strictly as any other lender would. For instance, you must make payments regularly and right on time or your RRSP can foreclose on you. You cannot give yourself a break on the mortgage rate either – it must be the market rate. There are administrative costs to pay as well. Remember too, that you can get a better return from many other investments and that you want to generate the best returns possible for your retirement fund.

Phase Four – The Peak Years: Arriving

During the years from 55 to 65, investors usually have an unprecedented opportunity to add to their nest eggs. Earnings should be at or near their peak while expenses – especially the ones required to raise a family – continue to dwindle.

From an investment viewpoint, this should be a time to top-up any financial plans. RRSPs should be maximized, and other tax savings plans initiated so that every dollar counts. Investments should be increasingly conservative. You are getting close to retirement and may not have the time to ride out a major down cycle in the market. If assets are large, plans for their distribution should be finalized.

At this point, those who have still not started a regular savings plan may decide to invest what little they have accumulated in risky, go-for-broke ideas. This is foolhardy. Few investments can really make up for lost time and any investments should be well considered. Losses should be taken seriously, as there's no time to allow for recovery. If funds for retirement do not look adequate at this point, now is the time to make contingency plans. What can you do after retirement that can provide you with the funds you need? How can you arrange your affairs now to ensure that you can carry out those contingency plans?

Phase Five – The Calmer Years: Retirement and Beyond

If you have followed the kind of plan we've touched on in this chapter, the post-retirement years will be less stressful. However, as regular expenses drop, new ones may appear. For many of us, working minimizes the idle time that could otherwise be spent on buying things. In addition, hobbies such as travelling, collecting, gardening and spending more time with family and friends can add up to more than you anticipated.

Your investments should include enough liquidity to provide for cash needs. Investments should be conservative, but not exclusively in fixed-income investments because of inflation. Inflation is the sworn enemy of anyone on a fixed income. Your returns should be monitored against inflation's erosive effects on a regular basis. The volatility of interest rates is another reason you should keep your assets diversified.

Measuring Your Tolerance for Risk

One more subject that should be discussed before we get into the planning process itself is risk. Risk is a popular topic in discussions about investments, but how can you gauge it? Try this litmus test – if you cannot sleep at night after buying an investment product, it's too risky for you. You may know people who have made money on penny mining stocks. But that doesn't mean you should, even if you can afford to lose your entire investment. Risk is a personal thing that you really must come to grips with yourself. Another way of gauging risk is by return. If an investment is touted as providing a 30% annualized return, guess what? There is risk involved – a great deal of risk.

Risk versus Return

To get an idea of the risk/return trade-off, consider treasury bills. You recall that T-bills are money market instruments issued by the Government of Canada. They can mature at various times, up to one year. By virtue of the fact that they are issued by the government, with its powers of taxation, these investments are considered risk-free. So as a starting point for returns, looking at the current yield on a T-bill will tell you what a risk-free investment is paying. From here it's all relative. But realize that you'll not get something for nothing. If someone offers you a return of 25% with no risk, you should run, not walk to the nearest exit. And if one GIC is paying a premium over another for the same period, ask yourself why. Perhaps one company needs five-year money to match its loan portfolio and is paying a premium to attract it. But if the rates across all terms are higher than those of other companies, the improvement in yield could really be a risk premium.

The Financial Planning Pyramid

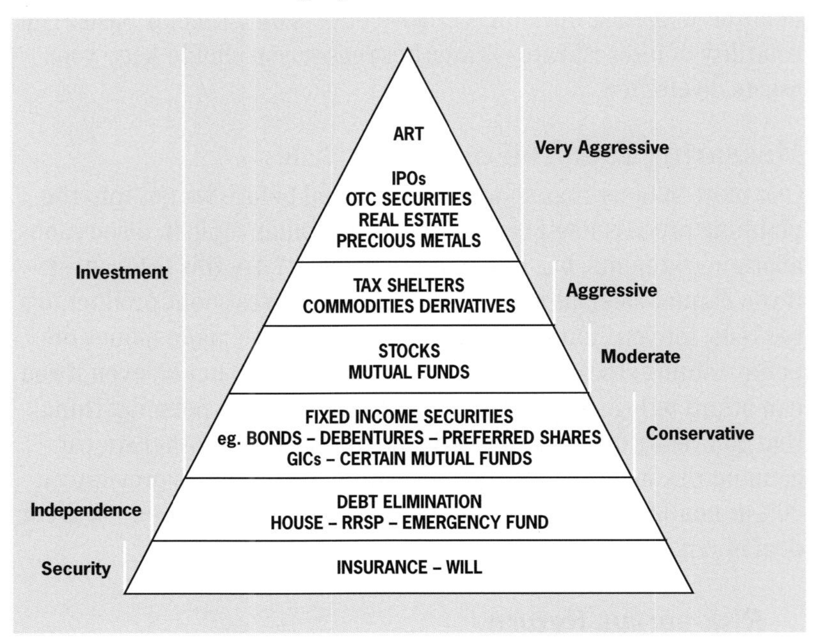

Another way of approaching the retirement planning process is to consider all your decisions within the context of a financial planning pyramid. The basic, most essential steps in the financial planning process – such as writing a will and buying adequate insurance – form the base of the pyramid. Higher layers contain more optional activities from starting a savings account to investing in futures. With regard to the different types of investments, there's one other thing you'll notice. The higher the level on the pyramid, the greater potential return and the higher degree of risk involved in that type of investment.

Let's have a quick look at each level of the pyramid:

Security

The base of the financial pyramid includes insurance and wills – two things that you and your family cannot afford to live without.

Insurance

Insurance is a financial planning tool and should not be thought of as a way of replacing a loved one with money. Consider the following scenario – one you might expect your friendly insurance agent to describe – about a young couple with five children. The wife has given up a lucrative career to stay home with the children at least for the next 12 or 13 years. The husband, hardworking, loving and reliable, is killed in a car accident, leaving an unemployed mate at home with the children, a mortgage and other bills to pay and no income and few assets. These stories tug at the heartstrings, but most people cannot see a connection between them and their own lives. Insurance forces people to consider their own death or disability, subjects we simply prefer not to talk about. Yet all your assumptions about financial planning assume that you'll be gainfully employed until your retirement. The purpose of insurance is to make sure those plans are realized even if you aren't able to do it yourself.

The Benefits of Life Insurance

Life insurance is an exceptional financial planning tool. In return for modest premiums, it can ensure that the lives of your loved ones go on as planned after your death. What's more, any death benefits paid by an insurance policy to a named beneficiary (but not an estate) are tax-free. Insurance creates an instant pool of money for your family to pay off debts like a mortgage, car and personal loans, as well as to fund educational costs for children. The only bad news is you won't be around to enjoy it yourself. So how much do you need?

To work out this figure, simply remove from your budget your income and any expenses pertaining to you specifically. The amount of insurance required would equal your contribution to the household.

For example, your earnings may cover a mortgage and a personal loan totaling $125,000, while you also pay monthly expenses of $1,000. You may decide to buy enough insurance to cover the debt outstanding as well as enough to generate an income of $1,000 a month for the miscellaneous expenses. That could mean you'll need approximately $250,000 in insurance.

Before you sign up for any insurance, read the information available on the policy to ensure that it's what you need, want, and can afford.

Calculating the amount of insurance and deciding what type to buy go hand in hand. A reputable life insurance agent or broker can walk you through the steps necessary to come to a decision. But remember, the commission paid to an agent on a whole life or permanent insurance policy is far greater than the commission paid on term insurance. At the same time, do not overlook benefits that may be available from work. Most companies provide term life insurance and sometimes make optional coverage available at favorable rates. This insurance may be convertible if and when you leave. Review this information before you buy extra coverage, and make the details available to the insurance sales person. Before you sign up for any insurance, read the information available on the policy to ensure that it's what you need, want, and can afford.

Disability Coverage is Essential

Personal disability insurance is a must for those unfortunate enough not to have this type of coverage through an employer. Insurance of this sort replaces income when you are suffering from a long term illness or disability. It can be expensive in comparison to life insurance and for that reason many otherwise well insured people don't bother with it. The fact is, however, that disability before the age of 65 is a lot more likely than death. For a 20-year old man, the chances of a disability of three months or longer are three times greater. For a 35-year old woman, the odds are seven to one. Disability policies come in many shapes and sizes so you should do some comparison shopping with the aid of an agent or broker.

Home Insurance

Whether you own or rent, home insurance is another coverage you cannot afford to be without. It covers a host of unfortunate occurrences including fire and other damage as well as lost or stolen property. It also provides liability coverage – the kind that comes in handy if a neighbor trips over the fence while trying to elude your dog.

As with other forms of insurance, cost varies depending on the amount and type of coverage you want. Three basic types of policies are offered – named perils, which covers only what's specifically mentioned in the policy; all risk, which covers you for anything that isn't specifically excluded in the policy; and comprehensive, which is an all-risk policy with fewer exclusions.

In addition, check to see if your insurance policy has a replacement value clause. This coverage ensures that you can replace your personal items at today's cost, not what you originally paid for them. It may not be important for electronics, which have generally declined in price over the past few years, but for clothes and other personal possessions, such a clause is worth the expense.

Wills Are a Must

A will is simply a necessity. While most people have a great deal of difficulty dealing with the inevitability of their own deaths, immortality isn't granted to those without wills. Leaving your family at the mercy of the court system is reckless. Each province has its own laws governing the situation of dying "intestate" or without a will. However, you can rest assured that there's no guarantee that anything resembling your wishes will be carried out upon your death. You need to tell people in advance how your assets should be disposed.

If you die without a will the official Guardian is appointed by the government.

Don't Leave it up to the Government

When you die without a will, the state steps in and decides what is best for your family. A portion of your assets would go to your spouse, with the balance passed on to your children, to be administered by the Official Guardian as appointed by the courts. If your spouse requires more money for the children from the estate, he or she must petition the courts to prove need. As well, investment decisions would be made by the Official Guardian. This in itself should scare you into preparing a will, for we all know how

Insurance: Term, Whole and Universal

There are two basic types of insurance – term insurance and whole life insurance.

Term insurance is temporary insurance that can provide protection for a limited time. It is inexpensive and is in essence a no-frills type of product. For some people, term is an adequate product that provides the coverage needed and no more. But term insurance does expire. The premiums for this type of insurance are not uniform – a 25-year old is going to pay a lot less than a 40-year old for the same amount of coverage. Because the need for insurance varies during your life, some people feel that term insurance is an appropriate choice – you can purchase large amounts when family responsibilities make the need for protection greatest, and then purchase smaller amounts with the same dollar premium at a later stage. For the disciplined financial planner, term does make sense, but for those who have difficulty saving, whole life insurance is a possibility.

Whole life is permanent insurance. It does not expire but rather will provide death benefits unless cancelled. The premium on the whole life insurance policy remains the same throughout its lifespan. The policy accumulates a cash surrender value, usually after five years, and can become an asset. A whole life policy can be borrowed against or used as collateral for a loan, so can be considered an investment. However, it doesn't stand up well on its investment merits alone – returns are generally poor.

Because term can replace whole life insurance, it is often suggested that it is better than whole life. Some financial pundits advise the investor to purchase term and put the difference between the price of term and whole life into a savings account. This is a good idea if it is done consistently.

Insurance companies have come up with a product that replicates this type of investment/insurance product. It is called universal life. This is a very flexible policy which really is a combination savings plan and life insurance policy. You pay a premium for the insurance and also deposit a sum of money into a savings account. The deposit and the premium can be very flexible, to suit an individual budget. They can be changed if necessary, as long as there is enough cash in the savings portion of the policy to pay for the life insurance premium. This is a great type of policy for certain individuals, and can be an effective estate planning tool.

well governments have managed their financial affairs in the last two or three decades. If you have no spouse or child, all assets would be transferred to surviving parents. Save your family or survivors a great deal of grief and prepare a will.

Independence

The next level of the pyramid involves buying a house and setting up your long-range retirement plans, as well as an emergency fund.

Wills

A will is a legal document that instructs your survivors how your affairs are to be settled after your death. It must contain certain information about you and it must name an executor, the person whom you charge with settling your affairs on your behalf. A will should be drawn up with the aid of a lawyer. Although a holograph will (one that is written in your own handwriting) can be valid as well, it is not recommended. One copy of the will usually remains in the possession of the lawyer; another copy kept with your financial information papers. The following is a partial list of the items that could be included in a will. If you are using a lawyer, prepare this information prior to your first meeting to ensure that none of your wishes are mistaken or left out altogether.

1) **The testator or person making the will must be clearly identified by name and complete address. All previous wills must be revoked.**
2) **The executor must be named. (Be sure to inform the person you have chosen. Better yet, discuss their willingness to take on this responsibility prior to springing it on them.)**
3) **Name a guardian for your children.**
4) **State any specific bequests or gifts, personal property or money.**
5) **Give instructions as to what to do with the remainder of the estate, e.g., does it pass on to your spouse or children?**

Some people also include instructions on the care of their children and how their guardian is to spend any monies for their education and upkeep. If the executor and guardians are well-chosen, there should be less need for detailed instructions. Flexibility for both of these parties is often more desirable than a rigid, difficult-to-administer estate that puts no faith in these people.

Setting up an Emergency Fund

An emergency fund is a pool of liquid assets in a savings account or near-cash equivalents. Financial planners have traditionally suggested the fund be equal to three to six months of living expenses, including mortgage payments, groceries, utilities, and other payables. This fund is for those worst-case scenarios: what if you became seriously ill for an extended period? Do you have disability insurance that would cover your drop in income and when does it kick in? If there is a problem in getting benefits due you, can you and your family survive until the money comes in? Being seriously ill brings with it enough hardship and suffering without having to wonder when your benefit plan will kick in. The emergency fund can see you through such dark periods. Another more commonplace happening in today's job market is a layoff or plant closure. While we have excellent social safety nets in Canada, it's wise to have some money put aside for a rainy day.

An emergency fund is a pool of liquid assets in a savings account or near-cash equivalents.

For some people, especially those with adequate insurance coverage, there may be better ways to manage your emergency fund. Accumulating three to six months' salary from after tax dollars can take a long period – time that you could otherwise use generating a better return on your savings. In some circumstances, it might make more sense to sock your savings away into RRSPs, capturing immediate tax benefits on your investment and putting your money to work sooner. If you do need access to such funds later, you'll be taxed as you withdraw them but presumably, your income level would be much lower. Investors who take this approach should also set up a line of credit for immediate access to funds in an emergency.

At the same time, it's best to eliminate any debts before advancing to the next steps in the pyramid. The one exception might be money borrowed to accumulate RRSPs. Most financial institutions lend money at or near prime for an RRSP investment. When you compare the value of the tax deduction you'll get to the cost of the loan, you'll be way ahead by borrowing. The key is to use your tax refund to pay off as much of the loan as possible.

Home Ownership

For most people, owning a house is more than just a lifestyle preference, it's one of the cornerstones of a sound financial plan. Historically, real estate has proved to be a solid investment with a rate of return in excess of inflation. Better yet, your home gets favorable tax treatment; any gain between the purchase and sale price of your home is tax-free. For these reasons, home ownership has traditionally been the most important part of the nest egg for most Canadians.

At the same time, you should realize that a house is probably the largest asset you'll ever own. The best approach is to take things slowly. Don't be talked into assuming too large a mortgage that you "can grow into". That may have made sense when incomes were rising rapidly and house prices were appreciating at a double digit pace every year, but those conditions no longer apply. If you overbuy, you run the risk of losing any equity you may put into the house. It's better to under-buy so that you can afford to save money for your retirement and comfortably pay living expenses. A modest, affordable home is certainly a better choice than a house that doesn't leave enough money to enjoy the rest of your life.

In fact, if you aren't emotionally attached to the idea of owning your home, you might be able to make a stronger case for investing in assets other than real estate. As a general rule you should compare monthly rental costs to the interest part of a monthly mortgage payment. The principal payments are thus the investment portion of the home ownership decision. The tradeoff to be evaluated then, is the difference between putting available funds into a home as a down payment versus investing in mutual funds and RRSPs. There are books and software programs to help you make your calculations, however, you'll have to make a lot of assumptions about future interest rates and rates of return.

Investments

The top section of the pyramid represents accepted wisdom on the levels of risk in other types of investment products. This is merely a representation though, and each investment should be reviewed on its own merits. For example, a deep discount or junk bond is nonetheless a bond, so it is considered within this table a conservative investment. In reality, junk bonds are extremely volatile and closer to an option purchase than a fixed income investment in terms of risk.

The Pyramid in Review

Let's review what we've accomplished so far. You have done your best to cover all the necessities of life to secure your family's welfare. This is the security base of the pyramid.

Second, you have built up cash reserves. Such reserves can include the house, RRSP, and an emergency cash fund for liquidity.

Last but not least is the growth part of your investment plan. If all goes well, here is where you can accumulate savings to fund the better things in life!

The Pyramid versus the Life Cycle

If you compare the levels of the pyramid to the life cycle approach we discussed at the beginning of the chapter, you may notice that they are contradictory in some respects. For example, a 20-year old can buy risky assets under the life cycle plan, but under the pyramid approach, that risk money would be channeled into an emergency fund.

It's important to remember that these are only guidelines. Sometimes the lure of a once-in-a-lifetime investment opportunity is too tempting to ignore. The pyramid is one approach to investing. It's a good one, as it's conservative and serves as a logical progression that makes use of available investment products. On the other hand, the life cycle approach is more like a series of signposts. How you fit these two pieces of the financial planning puzzle together is what will make your personal financial plan unique.

Reviewing Your Goals and Objectives

If you have been taking your financial plan seriously, you'll have developed a clearly defined list of goals or objectives. As we've said, writing your goals down lends a degree of urgency and importance to them. By giving you a track to run on, they make it easier to both reach your destination and measure your progress along the way.

You should have short, mid and long-term financial goals listed. Keep all your paperwork together; your written goals should be kept with your other financial information lists.

Writing your goals down lends a degree of urgency and importance to them.

An Annual Review is Important

Update all your records as well as your list of goals. Monitor your progress and make any necessary adjustments. Do not leave plans in place that are at odds with your goals. It's also a good idea to review your will and your insurance policies to ensure that these documents are still adequate and continue to reflect your wishes. It's amazing how easy it is to neglect such things in the face of dramatically changing circumstances.

What Can Go Wrong

There are many things that can disrupt a financial plan, natural disasters not included. These four are perhaps the most damaging.

- **Inflation** – is the enemy of bonds. Inflation implies a general rise in consumer prices and means that a dollar is just not a dollar any more. Equity investments offer protection against inflation. Fixed-income investments can too, provided the rate of return is higher than inflation. Always estimate the real rate of return on such investments, that is, the rate of return minus the rate of inflation.
- **Unemployment** – losing your job can be devastating. Emergency funds can help to ease financial problems.
- **Disability** – the proper insurance policy – company-sponsored or bought privately – can provide for your family's needs when you can't.

One final point. The single biggest reason financial plans fail is lack of follow-through. It does not matter how much planning you do if you shove it in a drawer and forget about it. To succeed, a financial plan is a living, breathing document. As we mentioned at the start, make sure your final plan is:

- do-able;
- flexible;
- easy to follow

If your plan can meet these criteria you should easily be on the way to financial success.

The Next Step

The next step is up to you. Hopefully, this book has given you a good foundation on which to build your investing activities. You may not feel ready to strike out entirely on your own, but you should be able to properly evaluate the information and advice that you get from various financial institutions. Whether you choose to operate on your own or work closely with an investment advisor, the knowledge you have acquired here will lead to better investment decisions and better results over the long term.

Remember, this is just the beginning. There is always more to learn. To help you do that, the bibliography in this book is full of suggestions for further reading as well as a list of investment information sources. We hope that all your investments will be fun, educational and profitable.

Summary

Although the range of investment possibilities is the same for everybody, your personal circumstances decide what will be attractive to you. This is why financial plans will vary from person to person.

In developing a financial plan, you must first know your current financial position. This means preparing a balance sheet and income statement for yourself. You can then use the life cycle approach to help you develop a suitable range of investments. There are some situations common to us all at certain stages of life, and the life cycle approach can be useful in putting together an appropriate investment strategy. Opening an RRSP is a suitable strategy at any stage, with the preferred time being earlier rather than later.

The financial planning pyramid can also be used to decide priorities. Insurance and will preparation form the base of the pyramid and should be attended to before moving up to the other levels. Buying a house, setting up an RRSP, putting aside emergency funds and reducing or eliminating debt form the next stage. Extra funds can then be used to generate investment growth.

Because a financial plan depends on personal circumstances that change over the years, the plan must be reviewed on a regular basis. At the same time, review your will and insurance policy. These documents will only work in your favor if they reflect your current circumstances and wishes.

SEDAR www.sedar.com

Barclays Global Investors www.iunits.com

American Stock Exchange www.amex.com

WebsontheWeb www.websontheweb.com

Yahoo! Finance http://finance.yahoo.com

Northernlight www.northernlight.com

Zack's Research www.zacks.com.

Carlson Online www.carlsononline.com

Globe Investor www.globeinvestor.com

Adobe www.adobe.com.

Edgar Web www.edgar-online.com

Industry Canada www.strategis.ic.ca

Statistics Canada www.statcan.ca

Index

G

H

I

K

L

M

N

O

T

U

V

W

Y

Z